IN MEMORY OF BORGES

Edited by Norman Thomas di Giovanni

· Jorge Luis Borges ·

· Graham Greene ·

· H. S. Ferns ·

· Alicia Jurado ·

· Mario Vargas Llosa ·

Foreword by Viscount Montgomery of Alamein

Constable London
in association with the Anglo-Argentine Society

First published in Great Britain 1988
by Constable and Company Limited
10 Orange Street London WC2H 7EG
The contributions are copyright respectively:
© 1988 Norman Thomas di Giovanni
© 1988 the Estate of Jorge Luis Borges
© 1988 Graham Greene
© 1988 H. S. Ferns
© 1988 Alicia Jurado
© 1988 Mario Vargas Llosa
© 1988 the Estate of Jorge Luis Borges
and Norman Thomas di Giovanni

Photoset in Linotron Sabon 11pt by
Rowland Phototypesetting Limited
Bury St Edmunds, Suffolk
Printed in Great Britain by
St Edmundsbury Press Limited
Bury St Edmunds, Suffolk

British Library CIP data
In memory of Borges.
1. Fiction in Spanish. Argentine writers.
Borges, Jorge Luis, 1899–1986. Critical studies.
I. Di Giovanni, Norman Thomas.   II. Borges, Jorge Luis, 1899–1986
III. Anglo-Argentine Society
863

ISBN 0 09 468370 0

CONTENTS

FOREWORD

The Anglo-Argentine Society has a number of praiseworthy objectives, perhaps the most important of which is to encourage good relations and better understanding between the people of Argentina and Great Britain. In 1981, under the chairmanship of Alan Tabbush, the idea was conceived to establish an annual lecture to be named after the illustrious Argentine writer Jorge Luis Borges, himself a living example of some of the Society's aims. After due consideration, discussion, and planning, preparations were sufficiently advanced for the inaugural lecture to be arranged for the autumn of 1982. The tragic conflict earlier that year in the South Atlantic, however, brought postponement, yet at the same time it gave an added reason for proceeding with the lectureship as a major part of the Society's contribution to the task of rebuilding the friendship formerly enjoyed by the two countries. Thus it was that the first lecture took place at the Royal Society of Arts, in London, on 5 October 1983.

Borges came to London for the event accompanied by his future wife, María Kodama, always his devoted supporter. It was a moving occasion but not without difficulty, for, in fact, no formal lecture was delivered. Instead, the great man had chosen to take questions and give spontaneous answers. Despite physical frailness, his clarity of thought, deep sincerity, and warm personality held the audience enthralled.

Borges approved the concept of an annual lecture and the ideas that lay behind it. He hoped that it would thrive and that one day its results would be published. A continuity of theme can be seen in the contributions of the editor and subsequent speakers; their efforts, although very different, are linked by the influence of Borges himself. This book – dare one say, the first of many – represents the fulfilment of his wishes.

Montgomery of Alamein
Isington Mill,
Alton, Hampshire
January 1988

EDITOR'S NOTE

This volume collects the first five Jorge Luis Borges lectures, a series of public addresses sponsored by the Anglo-Argentine Society of London and launched in the autumn of 1983 by Borges himself.

It should be pointed out that Graham Greene as well as Borges eschewed delivering a formal lecture. Both writers addressed themselves, after brief introductory remarks, to questions from their audiences. In his last years, Borges found this by far the easiest way to deal with his numerous speaking engagements the world over. It was what people wanted, anyway – the old master talking informally about his reading, his work, his habits, his life, and not pronouncing a prepared address on Shakespeare or Milton or gauchesco poetry. The public came not just to hear Borges but to see him, for he had a ready talent for entertaining as well as instructing those he spoke to. He was always witty and spontaneous, and his utterances came close to being conversations with his audience. A shy man, his blindness made public speaking, which terrified him, less of an ordeal; in fact, sightlessness, what he called his 'growing dark', simplified his task, freeing him of distraction, so that he could feel he was directing his words just to one person and not to a daunting multitude.

Occasionally, however, his blindness could give rise to bizarre occurrences or unintentional comic effects. Once, in Washington DC, when a microphone failed and no one had the wits to come forward and set matters right, he spoke for an hour with only the front row of a vast hall hearing a word he said. Occasionally, at the Royal Society of Arts, when questioners did not speak up enough and he was unable to hear all they said, he would answer not what was asked but what he thought was asked. In the end, his sweet nature always guaranteed that he won the day and his audiences' hearts, for in spite of the questions, or whether or not he heard them, his replies, as some of the following pages show, were always brilliant.

Graham Greene remarked that he was glad the Anglo-Argentine Society had agreed he was not required to give a lecture. 'I have never lectured in my life,' he told those who had come to listen to him, 'and I have also tried to avoid hearing lectures. At Oxford, I gave up going to lectures after my first term.'

Both men's contributions here were prepared from recorded transcripts. In Mr Greene's case, he kindly agreed to look over his remarks; Borges', however, have come under my scrutiny alone. I have relied on a long association with him and his work to have done them justice.

Jorge Luis Borges, whom I first met a little over twenty years ago, died in Geneva on 14 June 1986, a few months short of his eighty-seventh birthday. The introduction to this book, entered upon at the request of the publisher, takes the form of reminiscences, or a memoir. Concluding the volume is a translation of a prose poem by Borges about the futility of war in general and of one war in particular. He composed it in the momentous days of June 1982.

Appropriately, *In memory of Borges* makes its appearance on the anniversary of his death.

My personal thanks are due to the officers of the Anglo-Argentine Society, who were unstinting in their efforts to help in the preparation of this book: Alan Tabbush, the chairman who instituted the lectureship; Robin Majdalany, who succeeded him; Barney Miller, the current chairman; and George Gibson, the secretary. My thanks also to Viscount Montgomery, who recently retired as the Society's president, for contributing a foreword to the volume; and to Juan Eduardo Fleming, head of the Argentine Interests Section of the Brazilian Embassy, for his usual warmth and enthusiasm. And finally, for their cooperation and assistance, I wish to express my gratitude to Professor Ferns, Mr Greene, Mr Vargas Llosa, and to our publisher Robin Baird-Smith.

Norman Thomas di Giovanni
Gunn, Goodleigh, Devon
11 January 1988

IN MEMORY OF BORGES

Introduction by
Norman Thomas di Giovanni

There is an article, really a piece of photojournalism, in one of those Argentine weekly magazines, in which I can be seen walking down a Buenos Aires street with Borges leaning on my arm. Was the magazine *Siete Días* or *Gente*? That I no longer remember, but all the other details I am fairly clear about. It was 1969; we were walking east along Belgrano Avenue, crossing Santiago del Estero or more likely Salta, a block or two from the small flat where Borges was still living with his first wife. I am wearing my brown herringbone tweed suit and a tie, concessions to the demands of sober, formal Buenos Aires. We are crossing or about to cross Salta, Borges clutching my right arm in his somewhat frantic blind man's vice, and the large photograph in the magazine is a picture of me with him on my arm and definitely not the other way round – it is not a photograph of Borges being led along by some anonymous younger man, a foreigner, an American.

That year, on the dot of four every afternoon, five days a week, I picked Borges up from the Belgrano flat and, his arm firmly gripping mine, we walked the ten slow blocks east to the National Library, in Mexico Street, where our early evening's work awaited us. By this time, he had been Director of the Argentine National Library for fourteen years. The post, of course, was a sinecure. Borges was not a librarian, much less an administrator, and a loyal assistant director, José Edmundo Clemente, did the real work. Once or twice a month perhaps, like a ritual, a secretary came into the big office where Borges and I sat across from each other at a solid long mahogany table, and she would stand over a thick sheaf of papers, turning a corner of each page for him to initial. Whatever the bulk of paperwork, it never proved much of an interruption. Most of the time he initialled away while carrying on his discussion with me; but if things were going particularly well and he was in one of his playful moods, which were frequent, he might indulge in a bit of good-natured ribbing, poking fun at her to me in English or at me to her in Spanish.

'You see, di Giovanni, how mercilessly she makes me work.' Often the woman would be halfway out of the room before Borges would remember himself and, for form's sake, think to ask exactly what it was he had just signed.

'Only the usual accounts, Señor Borges,' she would say assuringly, the epitome of correctness and respect.

'Ah, yes,' he would rejoin, as if suddenly reminded of some immutable truth.

It was a game. The secretaries, one or two in the morning, a different one or two in the afternoon, hated troubling Borges about anything, especially when he was working, and to this day I am sure that even after it had been explained to him Borges never had the foggiest what he was signing.

'Borges,' I'd quip when the mood came over me, 'I can see from here that that sheaf you're putting your John Hancock to grants the whole library staff an extra two-week holiday with pay.'

And he would do a comic double-take, feigning astonishment, stop scribbling, look up trying to locate the secretary's face, and repeat my remark in Spanish to her.

'*No, jamás nunca, Señor Borges; le juro.*' And with her oaths to the contrary and not-on-your-lifes, he let himself be readily convinced every time.

This is not to suggest that Borges did not take the job in earnest. He did. But at the same time he knew he was a figurehead – a mere figurehead, he would have phrased it – and, never pompous about anything, he allowed himself to be ironic about the post. Deep down, he was proud of the library, of the position, and grateful for it too. Almost in the manner of a credulous child, he would recite for visitors that the library contained 800,000 volumes. Or later, 900,000. It was one of the few facts Borges ever had at his fingertips. To him facts were the antithesis of the essence of truth, and he found them meaningless. This was the only fact I can remember his spouting that required – unlike the year of his birth, say – frequent updating. The job was the perfect symbol for him, and he was the perfect symbol for the job. Indeed, what country in the world would not have rejoiced having a Borges as its titular head? He performed the office like a master – not as if he had been born to it, but because he had been born to it.

Those evenings of ours were devoted to the translation of stories, poems, and essays of his into English. 'My afternoons now are usually given over to a long-range and cherished project,' Borges was to write a year later, when he was seventy-two. 'For nearly the past three years, I have been lucky to have my own translator at my side, and together we are bringing out some ten or twelve volumes of my work in English, a language I am unworthy to handle, a language I often wish had been my birthright.'

As the young man from *Siete Días* or *Gente* knew, then, all this made a good story: the Yank from Boston who had suddenly popped up and was shepherding the legendary Borges along the streets of Buenos Aires and working with him at the National Library. In fact, the story had a bit of every-thing – the exotic and the homely. Here was the lofty National Treasure, for whom New York publishers were competing, for whom they had sent one of their own to the ends of the earth to watch over. It proved Borges really was a world figure and not just an oddball local, an Anglophile with a passion for books; it meant that Buenos Aires and Argentina counted in the world for something more than excellent steaks and crack football players. It was a fine tonic for the constant doubt about his identity that assails the *porteño* at the best of times. These were not the best of times. 'Nationalism is creeping in all the time,' Borges sneered. It was the military dictatorship of General Onganía; soon grim-faced Federal police, more of them every week, would be appearing on street corners wearing jackboots and nasty submachine guns; soon the faithful flock would be bleating for the return of Perón. With the horizon fast shading from leaden to black, enter the young Yank in the tweed suit who had something in common with half the population of Buenos Aires – a comforting Italian surname. Which was why the story was about me, why the pictures were of me with the National Treasure on *my* arm and not of Borges with me on his.

I often kidded him about this. As we moved through Florida Street, a pedestrian precinct on the way to his mother's, people would open a way, turn round, gape, point. 'It never ceases to amaze me the way strangers seem to recognize me,' I would tell him, deadpan. ' "Look," they say, "there's di Giovanni – there, with the old man on his arm." ' It made him laugh every time. The passers-by never failed to greet him; some even held their children up for him to touch. He always asked people their names, where they were from. Ah, yes. He had a friend there. A lawyer and a fine poet named Fernández Ordóñez. Borges was a living monument, and the Argentines revered him.

At the library we shuffled through the revolving door and up the grand marble staircase, entering first the outer office with the scruffy, bare, wooden floor, where the secretaries huddled at a tiny table in the corner by the window. Lightless except by that window. Bare and spartan. A small wire wastebasket beside the table. The one telephone, big, clumsy, black, its cord frayed. It didn't matter. The phones, like the secretaries, only worked part-time. The building dated from 1901 and had been, as Borges was fond of telling visitors, the seat of the national lottery. The inner sanctum, Borges' office, had an extraordinarily high ceiling, green wallpaper printed with bamboo-like fronds, polished mahogany panelling and a parquet floor. We worked at the old-fashioned conference table in the centre of the room. At the far end was the desk that Paul Groussac, a distinguished predecessor, had had built to his own design. It was U-shaped. If you sat behind it, as Borges never did, it surrounded you. It had strange drawers and odd compartments. Borges later described it briefly at the end of his story 'There are More Things'.

The room's other furnishings were a couple of revolving bookshelves and a tall set of drawers where Borges slipped the drafts of poems he dictated in the morning to a secretary. Two pairs of doors led off the room straight onto a corridor. These we used only when trying to give the slip to someone who might be waiting in the outer office or when we went to the vast, stark loo that was used only by us. Next door was the room Groussac had died in, a detail Borges took ghoulish delight in recounting. For once upon a time the director had lived in. There were traces of a kitchen that proved it. But Elsa, the new Mrs Borges, whom Borges had married at sixty-eight (she was some ten or twelve years younger), would have none of it. She was right, of course. The library was a gloomy place, and I thought I too would go blind there. There was a dictionary of the Spanish Royal Academy, whose paper and binding Borges and I were fond of smelling, on the main table. The one place in all Buenos Aires where the tweed suit was no match for the winter was in the dank cavern of Borges' office. But there was a large, ornate fireplace at my back, where a fire of eucalyptus logs would glow. Not burn but glow; if I backed up to it now and again, the icy chill was momentarily dispelled. Still, one was thankful for small mercies.

What the photographs in the magazine article do not show is the crablike walk I had developed, much to the detriment of my lower back muscles. Buenos Aires pavements are narrow, and to negotiate them with Borges on my right arm I had to learn to master the art of walking with my left hip and left arm leading the way. To make matters worse, my extended left hand always carried a briefcase bulging with papers and books. There I was with the National Treasure on my arm, keeping him safe from the murderous traffic, the ubiquitous excavations, and the broken tiles of the city's pavements, steering him round open pits or dodging beau traps. And all the while the squat buses inched along in step with us, throbbing and belching thick black exhaust over the Treasure; over my herringbone tweed; over his monologue about Victoria Ocampo, whom he dubbed Queen Victoria for her imperial ways, or Ernesto Sábato, dubbed the Dostoyevsky of Santos Lugares for his bouts of melancholia; over an example of the word music of Dunbar, Coleridge, or the Bard himself, whose 'multitudinous seas incarnadine', capped with 'making the green one red', never failed to rouse and thrill Borges – potholes, pitfalls, grime, soot, lethal traffic, and sputtering buses be damned.

Once, fourteen years later and forty miles away across the river in Uruguay, in the town of Colonia, where I was helping make an Arena film about Borges, I stumbled across a half-open gateway that gave a glimpse of a picturesque garden with a big fig tree ripening in the middle of it. I couldn't resist. In I strolled as though the place were mine. Immediately a man dashed out of a house, a stern look on his face, to halt me in my tracks.

'*Le felicito,*' I said in my most winning Spanish, trying to disarm him. 'I congratulate you; your garden is a jewel.'

He drew up to me, tall, handsome, almost sneering, an obvious *porteño*. Then the belligerence drained from his look.

'*Yo te conozco a vos,*' he said straight out, launching into the familiar. 'I saw you walking down Calle Florida in 1969 or 1970 with Borges on your arm.'

There are jottings in a series of diaries, the old War Resisters League peace calendars I was partial to at the time, in which I chronicled those first teeming weeks in Buenos Aires after I arrived there in the middle of November 1968. Despite the suffocating heat, Borges was tireless in showing me the hospitality in his country that he had thanked me for showing him in mine when we had parted in Cambridge, Massachusetts, seven months before.

He and Elsa met my plane at Ezeiza on the night I got there and whisked me straight to the modest hotel she had found for me in the Avenida de Mayo, a short walk from their flat. The next day, after lunch with them, Borges could barely wait to show me the National Library and a few spots nearby on the old south side of the city that he both worshipped and had turned into myth. A house from the previous century; a grilled archway; a long street of low houses; a dusty park. 'After all, these places mean a great deal to me; they're my past.' It was touching the way he apologized for the absence of grandeur or glamour he thought that I, as a Bostonian, had a right to expect. But that was politeness. Beneath the courtesy, you were aware of his intense personal pride.

We began work at the library the next morning, a Saturday, when the library was closed, for that had been the pact. I would not come as a tourist; I would only come if we could continue what we had begun at Harvard during the months we had known each other there. The diary for 1968 records that we busied ourselves on his poem 'Heraclitus'.

That same day he introduced me to a student of his, María Kodama, whom he was to marry sixteen and a half years later, only weeks before his death. And that night, my second full evening in Argentina, he took me to dine at the home of Adolfo Bioy Casares, where I was presented to some of Borges' closest friends. This was an event I had been looking forward to for months; from the warmth of the reception I received from Bioy and his wife, Silvina Ocampo, Borges had talked to them about me. Bioy and Silvina were both writers – he of novels and stories, she of stories and poems (she was also an accomplished artist who had studied with De Chirico) – and together they and Borges had collaborated on a variety of literary projects. Manuel Peyrou, the novelist, was also there, and towards the end of the meal Teddy Paz, one of the younger literati, ambled in. That evening, that dinner, was truly auspicious, but not just for me because it marked the start of four enduring new friendships. Bioy got his car out and drove us home at one a.m. By then something had happened to make it one of the most important evenings in Borges' life.

During those final weeks of his stay in Cambridge, where he had been delivering the 1967–68 Charles Eliot Norton Lectures and we had been preparing an English edition of his selected poems, we had read together and chosen and made literal drafts of dozen upon dozen of Borges' sonnets, a form he increasingly favoured, since he could easily write them in his head. I knew that. But it did not keep me from wearying of those same fourteen hendecasyllabic lines, the inevitability of those seven pairs of rhymes. The very constriction, in fact, was giving me claustrophobia. I told him so – not that it would alter the shape of our project in any way. I told him simply because I saw no one else come forward, even once, and tell him the truth. Every poem, tale, or essay he had ever written was hailed a masterpiece; each of his utterances, on whatever subject, seemed to have cast a spell over academics the length and breadth of America. To me, he confessed his fears, his inadequacies. He felt he would never write again; so did America. Borges' isolation was cruel, crippling, and complete. He was high up on a pedestal, a monument.

He listened and explained, by rote, that sonnets were all he could now manage. He was not vehement, nor was I. I simply reminded him by their titles of some fine poems written during his blindness that were not sonnets, and no more was said. But within a month or two of his return to Buenos Aires, Elsa began posting me at regular intervals a series of poems that were new and fresh – and not a sonnet among them. By the time I reached Buenos Aires, I was in possession of seventeen uncollected poems.

'Are these all recent poems, or is this work you found in some bottom drawer?' I asked him on the morning we tackled 'Heraclitus'.

'Why?' he said in a panic. 'Don't you like them?'

'They're marvellous.'

'Ah, that's a relief,' Borges said. 'You see, I was doing what you told me to do back in Cambridge.'

'Yes, and it means you have half a new book here.'

'No, no!' he protested, flying into a rage. 'I won't publish another book. I haven't published a new book in eight years, and I won't be judged by this stuff.'

He was beside himself in a way I had never seen before. It was a hot potato, and I let it drop.

But over dinner the next night at Bioy's he blurted out aggressively, 'Di Giovanni has a crazy idea. He wants me to publish a new book of poems.' It was the manner he used, I was to learn, when he found himself on unsure ground but wanted to give the opposite impression.

'But, Georgie,' Bioy immediately chimed in, chuckling his infectious little chuckle. 'That seems to me a splendid idea.'

Silvina agreed; Peyrou agreed. I had no need to add a word.

One day the next week, there was an unexpected phone call from Borges, with a hint of mystery in his voice, saying he had an errand to run that morning and would I meet him at the library a bit later on. When around midday we eventually got together again, he was jubilant. 'I've been to see Frías,' he said. Carlos Frías was his editor at Emecé. 'I told him, "Frías, I want to publish a new book of poems."' Again the aggressive tone.

'Let me guess his decision,' I said, playing the straight man. 'He accepted.'

Borges was stunned and momentarily deflated. 'Yes. How did you know?'

That did it. His mind was made up. He was writing a new book and he wanted everyone to know he was writing a new book. 'Thirty-four poems, eh? You think that's about right, do you? That's the figure I gave Frías. Now you're sure we have seventeen. Let's go over that list of yours once again.'

We went over the list, which he learned by heart, ticking each title off on his fingers. What this meant, I told him, was that from then on we would work together only in the afternoons. He must devote his mornings to dictating new work. Borges offered no demurrer.

That was a skirmish. The real battle loomed ahead – the bits of evidence are there in the diary jottings – but I would not be aware of this for another six months. The entry for 4 December 1968 tells that in the evening we went out to Palermo, the neighbourhood of Buenos Aires where Borges had grown up, and we walked around the streets before going around the corner to eat *empanadas* at the home of Elsa's cousin Olga.

'Don't expect anything now,' Borges had prefaced the journey in his characteristic way.

It was a year and a day since we had first met. We stopped at an old *almacén*, where two men played with a pack of greasy cards at a plain wooden table. The place was ill-lit and nearly empty. Borges asked for a couple of *cañas quemadas*, an old-fashioned rum-like liqueur. Afterwards, outside, he confessed, 'I asked for a small one because a big one would have defeated me.' He told me he hadn't been out this way for thirty years. Then, like an eager schoolboy, he showed me a narrow, cobbled alleyway, pointing out that it was untypical for running in a diagonal instead of forming the side of a square. And on the spot he began recounting the 'plot of a story that has the ghost of Juan Muraña as a protagonist.' (An entry in a pocket notebook tells me this.) But of course he at once lamented the fact that, though he might still compose poems, he would never set down this story, since there was no way he could ever manage to write prose again. I gave him a sympathetic ear.

He and Elsa were invited to Israel for a few weeks early in the new year, and he came back full of wry little stories about the Holy Land. The Israelis, one notebook jotting tells me, were 'a bunch of Russians or Germans in disguise, playing at being characters out of the Old Testament. Noahs.' But he was elated. He was working, which in Borges' terms meant justifying his existence. And, what was more, harder than ever before in his life. (This was Bioy's observation; he had close to forty years' experience of Borges' habits.) Mornings were spent working on new poems for his book, dictating them to a secretary. In February, our afternoons were given over to a translation and rewriting of the long series of miniature essays that made up *The Book of Imaginary Beings*. By then I had burned my bridges and decided to stay on in Argentina longer than the five months I had initially planned. We finished the *Imaginary Beings* on 20 May 1969; Borges was so delighted with the result that any future translation of the book, he insisted, must be based on our English version. He also insisted that we now celebrate the end of the job by writing some new pieces for the book directly in English. We concocted four, working into them all manner of silly things, like the long Dutch name of one of my friends, a family surname, and my Buenos Aires street and flat number. It was all in good fun and the kind of thing Borges took glee in. Three days later, we wrapped the book up with a new foreword; three days after that, the typescript was winging its way to New York.

'*Norteamérica*,' Borges told the pillarbox, giving it an affectionate pat. 'I always tell the box where the letter goes. Otherwise, how would it know?'

The jotting in the peace calendar for this year tells that on 11 June Borges and I had worked on pages 17–19 of his 1951 short story 'Ibn Hakkan al-Bokhari, Dead in His Labyrinth', and that that evening we took a taxi out to his publishers in the two thousand block of Alsina to turn in the last poem of his new book *Elogio de la sombra* – *In Praise of Darkness*. An emendation added later in brackets records that 'more material was turned in after this date.' This was his fifth book of poems, he was to write in his foreword to the volume later that month, and to 'the mirrors, mazes, and swords which my resigned reader already foresees, two new themes have been added: old age and ethics.' As it turned out, there was something else in the book too – a grain of sand that would make a pearl. This was a story, not a prose poem, no more than three or four pages long about a man who hides out in a cellar for nine years.

Borges' lament about not being able to write down short stories that he was forever working out in his head did not end after our Palermo excursion. Over the next months, they became a more and more frequent topic of conversation on our walks to and from the library. At some point – but this was much later on – I began keeping track of them; by then the list I drew up numbered eight. That autumn (it was the southern hemisphere) I no longer just lent a silent ear but began a subtle campaign of egging him on, shoring up his confidence, and proving to him that his writing days were far from over. I had two arrows in my quiver. One was the five-page story 'The Intruder' that he had dictated to his ancient mother three years earlier; the other was the recent 'Pedro Salvadores', the man in the cellar.

'Sure you can,' I'd point out. 'After all, the difference in length between "The Intruder" and any of your other stories is a bare page or two.'

This was a slight exaggeration, perhaps, but he never opposed the argument. On the contrary, my persuasiveness made him open up, and he began using me as a sounding board for yet another tale whose plot he now wove aloud to me. And he'd ask my opinion of specific elements – should he add another incident? Were the main characters different enough?

I never tried to supply answers but would raise more questions. 'What are the alternatives?' I kept wanting him to tell me.

He'd ponder, come up with something, and we'd kick it around. I knew he was girding himself and working up to something; and I was determined to feed his mood whilst not letting him off the hook.

Then, at his doorstep: 'No, I fear it's too late in the day; I don't think I could manage it.'

'Tommyrot,' I'd say. His Edwardian slang, as I called it, was one of our pet jokes. 'Why not try? It's a good story. It's only a matter of writing "Pedro Salvadores" twice. Eight pages. You can do it.'

And on and on it went for several weeks. One day, in the midst of this, Manuel Peyrou rang from *La Prensa*, where he worked as an editor, to tell Borges that the paper was celebrating its centenary later in the year and was inviting every Argentine writer of note to contribute to a succession of special Sunday supplements. Here was another turning point. Not long after this, Borges took a poem around to them. But the next day, rather than feeling good about it, he was actually glum.

'I don't think a poem's what they had in mind,' he said.

'What do you mean?'

'I think they'd like a story.'

'Of course they'd like a story. We'd all like a story. Why not write them one?'

I never for a moment believed *La Prensa* was unhappy with his poem; certainly Peyrou knew that Borges had more or less given up writing stories since 1953. This was Borges having a pang of conscience. *La Prensa* had offered him the same fee whether they got a poem or a story out of him, and he felt he had cheated them. Whatever the truth of the matter, the mysterious strands were coming together fast now.

It became an open secret at the library that Borges was dictating a full-length short story; he knew I knew, but superstitiously he refused to breathe a word of it to me. He didn't have to, as the team of secretaries gave me daily reports. It went through two or three drafts and took him two or three weeks to write. He finally came clean when he'd finished, but he made no offer to show me the result. I bided my time.

A few days later I lied and told him I was short of money. Reaching for the billfold he kept in his inside breast pocket, he asked how much I needed. No, I laughed, what I had in mind was the new story, which I wanted to translate and sell to *The New Yorker*, where our work had been appearing. This took place on a Monday. All right, he said, but not that day. I would have to wait until Friday.

There was no earthly reason for his not handing me the story then and there, except that as the remote possibility did exist that Friday might never come round he could actually trick himself into believing he would escape having to stand judgement. It was complicated; it was capricious; it was Borges.

But that Friday did come round – according to my diary it was 16 May – and the delivery could be put off no longer. After our afternoon's ration of *Imaginary Beings* and just before we knocked off, he put the typescript in my hands, saying, 'Don't read it until Monday; we'll talk about it then.' I suppose it was one last desperate try; maybe he thought he'd have better luck and Monday would never happen.

The story was 'The Meeting', a marvellous tale set back in 1910 about two well-off young men who quarrel over cards and fight a duel with knives in which one of them dies. At the same time, on the fantastic side, the story is about the secret life of the weapons the men had chosen. I found it remarkably polished, and the draft contained only a couple of minor flaws. One was that in the dark, in a house without electric light, two characters begin studying a cabinet that houses a collection of old knives.

'That's easy,' Borges said as we worked out the translation. 'We'll have one of them light a lamp.' And on the spot, in English, he dictated a line to correct the lapse. My diary entries record that on 3 June I worked very late typing up 'The Meeting' for *The New Yorker*, and that at the library the next evening Borges and I translated the bits of new material into

Spanish and inserted them into a set of galley proofs that we then delivered to *La Prensa*, where Peyrou gave each of us a copy of his latest novel *El hijo rechazado*.

Within three weeks we heard from Robert Henderson at *The New Yorker* that they were taking 'The Meeting', and the news had a dramatic effect on Borges. In fact, nothing could have done more just then to send his confidence soaring. In July, on the seventeenth and eighteenth, I read page proofs of *Elogio de la sombra* to Borges, then read through them a second time alone. I corrected fresh proofs on the twenty-eighth. The book was published to great acclaim in August, on Borges' seventieth birthday. Three days earlier, on the evening of the twenty-second, Emecé gave the book an extravagant send-off on a stage in the Galería Van Riel, where one Dr E. Molina Mascías (whoever he was) spoke at some length, and the *'primera actriz'* (whatever that means) María Rosa Gallo and the *'primeros actores'* (ditto) Enrique Fava and Luis Medina Castro read a large number of the poems. The place was packed out and a bit of a circus. On the copy of the book he gave me the day before, Borges had written, '*Al colaborador, al amigo, al* promesso sposo,' for in a few days' time I was to be married. On the Sunday, his birthday, Elsa threw a little party at home with a cake iced in blue and white in the shape and colours of the book itself. You could even read the title on it. It was not at all Borges' style but he was nonetheless radiant. The next day was the wedding, with Elsa and Borges as the official witnesses at the registry office, and with her sister Alicia Ibarra and cousin Olga and Teddy Paz as extras. Poor Elsa, she was obliged to throw a second party in two days – this one for the promessi sposi. Silvina Ocampo and Manuel Puig were there; so was *Elogio de la sombra* – not the book but the cake, or, rather, what was left of it. Plus the wedding cake. By then, though, quite sensibly, Borges had had enough and did not attend. Instead, he went to work at the library.

After that, it all became a whirlwind. In October, two days before 'El encuentro' appeared in *La Prensa*, Borges finished another new story, the one called 'Rosendo's Tale', in English; the day we completed the translation of it we delivered the original to *La Nación*. Now the work found its way into my hands as soon as he finished it. In November came 'The Unworthy Friend', which we took with us to translate in the United States while Borges was lecturing at Oklahoma and where we gave readings and talks at a number of other universities. 'Juan Muraña', the story he had told me about the year before on the very spot where it was set, was finished in mid-January. There was no stopping him now. 'The Duel' came next, but before he put the finishing touches to it he began dictating 'The End of the Duel'. He long since knew he was doing the impossible – writing a new book of stories. On 3 March he finished 'Guayaquil' and on the fifth began 'Doctor Brodie's Report'. The day he finished 'Brodie' he began 'The Gospel According to Mark', completing the first draft of it in under a week. The only hiccup came when he had reached the eight mark. By then he was so anxious to see the collection in print that he ran out of patience. Not of stories, thank goodness, but of patience. He had another three in mind but he simply couldn't wait. As the completed stories were very short, a book of them would have come to no more than seventy pages, and I considered that a mistake. He had been invoking Kipling and the *Plain Tales from the Hills* as a kind of model for his brevity; I pointed out, however, that *Plain Tales* ran to over three hundred pages and contained forty stories. It was no use; he was going to see Frías to tell him he wanted to publish a book of eight stories. And off he went.

I picked up the phone, got Frías, and explained the situation. 'Say no to him,' I told the publisher. 'Tell him he's got to write at least three more. They're there in his head but he's just being lazy.'

Frías saw that I was right. Borges came back and told me that Emecé wanted another three stories. To his credit, he didn't sulk over the news for even a second. Sulking, like self-pity, was never Borges' pigeon. Instead, he immediately set to work writing the three required stories, probably counting his blessings that he had three more stories to tell. I never told him about my intervention. We set about re-reading and ordering the book-length typescript in mid-April, a week later he turned it in, and *El informe de Brodie* was published early in August. By any standard, it was a remarkable achievement; by his own, it was nothing short of a miracle. After nine years without writing a book, he had now, within twelve months, written two.

Like Turner, a painter he admired, Borges in his old age also set out to fashion something new, freer, more personal. In many ways he succeeded; undeniably, the prose of his late work is less cluttered and more responsible. In short, better written. He felt that at last he had found his voice. Six more volumes of poetry were to follow *In Praise of Darkness*; seventeen more short stories followed *Doctor Brodie's Report*.

'I no longer regard happiness as unattainable,' he said bravely on reaching seventy-one.

That year, there were no celebrations when the book came out, and certainly there was no cake. Somewhat sadly, that had all changed.

There are among my papers two spiral-bound notebooks with ruled pages, workbooks I called them, in which I took down from his dictation on sixty-four recto leaves the story of Borges' life. As far as I am aware, this autobiography is the single most extensive piece of writing Borges ever committed to paper. Like much else that we did, it too seems to have been born of a series of accidents or obstacles – unforeseen and unforeseeable events that somehow or other, uncannily, we kept turning to advantage.

With *The Book of Imaginary Beings* in print and a number of the recent stories and poems beginning to appear in American magazines, Borges and I itched for a chance to present in our own versions a selection of his older stories, the ones on which his fame rested. Of course, we would have preferred being allowed to translate the seventeen stories of his best book, *El Aleph*, written in the very rich period between 1945 and 1953, but a competing publisher, who claimed rights to about half these tales, prevented us from doing so. Our own publisher, however, the understanding and very accommodating Jack Macrae, was not averse to obliging us. So by begging, borrowing, and nearly stealing – that is, given the chance, we would have stolen – Borges and I were able to map out the volume that eventually appeared in the autumn of 1970 as *The Aleph and Other Stories 1933–1969*.

The exercise in autobiography had twofold roots. The first of them was in the vexing problem just described, when Borges was denied the right to determine the form and fate of his own work. As our compromise volume took shape, I grew more and more convinced that it needed something more than just our spanking translations if we were to avoid hoodwinking the public with yet another anthology of Borges' work.

The second part of these roots and the story is a happier affair and even funny. At the University of Oklahoma, several months earlier, I had been able to prevail upon Borges – not without great difficulty – to conclude his set of six lectures on Argentine literature by talking about himself. But on the afternoon of that final lecture he was in a blue funk. He had never before spoken about his own work publicly – it would never have occurred to him to indulge in such a pointless, immodest activity – and it was late in the day, and why on earth, and he simply was not going to be able to go through with it, etc. I saw I had a full-scale panic on my hands. By some strange chemistry, however, his panics always managed to turn the blood in my veins to ice water. It was a partnership, after all, and one of us had to be steady at all times. After our customary afternoon naps – his sleepless and unrefreshing, he claimed – I could see how pent up he was, so I suggested a walk. Our hotel stood about three-quarters of a mile from the campus on what seemed to be the edge of Norman, Oklahoma, where it occupied the corner of a perfectly square block. Arm in arm, Borges and I slowly circumnavigated that block. Once.

'Just remember your Dickens,' I told him. Twice.

'*David Copperfield*,' I told him, '"I was born on a Friday, at twelve o'clock at night."' And three times.

'Nothing fancy, now. You're telling a story, that's all there is to it.'

Every once in a while, Borges' lips began to move. 'I was born in Buenos Aires, in 1899,' he mumbled.

'That's the hang of it,' I said.

He was unconvinced. I couldn't tell him, but so was I.

Of course, he did marvellously, his audience loved it, and our Oklahoma sponsors, Lowell Dunham and Ivar Ivask, were duly pleased. Three months later in Buenos Aires, recalling the little triumph, I had a brainstorm and asked them at Norman to provide us with a transcript of the talk. I wrote to Macrae to tell him that we'd hit on an idea to beef up the book: we would add to it Borges' story of his own life, written directly in English. The lecture, I knew, would come to around twenty pages; I figured that with a few days' work we'd be able to flesh it out to thirty. So carried away was I that somewhere along the line I promised Jack we'd provide the book with a kind of appendix as well, also to be written in English, in the form of commentaries on each of the book's twenty stories. I knew that readers were having difficulty with Borges; worse, I knew that the universities kept him swathed in unnecessary mystery. At the same time, since his stories were really all about himself, his various guises, and dimensions of his thought, what better setting for them by way of introduction than the story of his life?

The pages from Oklahoma reached us some time in April 1970. By then, we had most of the stories translated and seemed to be on target. But reading the transcript of the lecture, my heart dropped down into my shoes. The talk started out like *David Copperfield*, all right, but it soon went jumping all over the place without order or logic. Sick with worry, I explained the predicament to Borges, for some reason or other fearing a negative response on his part. Instead, undaunted, and paraphrasing one of his favourite authors – English and nineteenth-century, of course – he said, 'Fling it aside and be free! We'll start over again from scratch.'

We did. On 21 April, the day after the typescript of *El informe de Brodie* went off to Emecé, we pitched in. That first day I took down five pages. I was prepared this time. I made us outline the material beforehand, breaking his life down into manageable chunks, chapters, of which we ended up with five. I made him stick to that outline. 'No, no, don't jump ahead to your mother; let's get it all down about your father and his family first and then we'll tackle her.' It went like that. The next day, I took down five more pages; the day after that, six. At this rate, it was going to come out longer than hoped for, which was all to the good. And better than anything, it looked like being a piece of cake.

On the fourth day, there was a flood of visitors to see Borges at the library and he had a lecture to give at seven o'clock. 'No work done,' says the diary entry. The following week started with permission coming from Grove Press to allow us to make new translations of two vital stories, so we immediately tackled them, since it would permit Macrae to send a good portion of the typescript to the printer while Borges and I worked on. But alas! it was not to be so simple. What with the two translations to get out, a steady stream of visitors from abroad plaguing me, and Borges giving lectures on what seemed every other night, we got not one jot further on the story of his life until 16 May. That day we were down to three and a half pages, and it was not much good.

The fact of the matter was that Borges' mind was on something else. It was at this point that he said to me, 'I've committed what seems to me now an unaccountable mistake, a huge mistake. A quite unexplainable and mysterious mistake.'

He was, of course, referring to his rocky marriage to Elsa, and he was in a pit of despair. It was significant that 16 May was a Saturday. We hadn't worked together on weekends for a very long time, yet here we were once more at the National Library. And it was not because of our deadline with Macrae – it was because Borges could no longer bear life at home. My diary records that on two days that week Borges had been too distraught for us even to attempt any work. What he needed was to talk about his private life, a thing that was so completely unlike him it only drove home to me the depths of his misery. Most of what he told me I already knew. He poured it out; I listened.

That Saturday was another turning point, for in the afternoon I invited a friend of ours, a lawyer from Córdoba who was in town that week, to tea at the Molino, the big old-fashioned *confitería* by the Congress that he was fond of. Two days later, he and I and Borges went to consult a friend of mine, a local lawyer. Between these two legal minds a bleak picture was painted. For starters, there was no divorce as such under Argentine law – only a form of legal separation that everyone referred to as divorce and that was as effective as any divorce but that did not allow for remarriage.

The next six weeks were an agony of hell. As far as I could, I carried on with the autobiography by myself, typing up whatever dictation we had completed, doing the necessary background research, and checking facts and dates. One Saturday we actually managed to revise half the first chapter. But the next was devoted to drawing up a list of Borges' marital grievances for the Córdoba lawyer. It was not until 28 May that the opening chapter was finished; not until 9 June that we had rewritten the second. We had begun working Sundays now too. But the trouble was that in addition to the delicate, surreptitious work on the legal front – endless meetings with a team of lawyers, countless errands and researching on their behalf – at one and the same time we had too many other matters clamouring for our attention. There were the proof-sheets of *El informe de Brodie* to read. That stole three or so days' time, and on the heels of that four more days were lost when we had to produce, in English, a thousand-word introduction to an encyclopaedia article for Grolier, the New York publisher, which was at least a year overdue. Macrae, getting understandably nervous, wanted to publish the stories without any of the new material, but I lied through my teeth and wrote him that all was coming along fine. It was. What I failed to say was fine – but at a snail's pace.

Meanwhile, I sent the first chapter of the autobiography to Henderson at *The New Yorker*, asking whether he thought they might be able to use it. He replied at once to say that if the rest were as good, yes. The entire week of 15 June is blank in my diary with only an explanatory scribble, 'no work on auto. essay this week. Spent most of time preparing the divorce.' The next month started out with blank pages as well.

D-Day was 7 July 1970. Only it was not an invasion but a getaway. That chill, grey winter's morning – as part of our elaborately hatched plan – I lay in wait for Borges in the doorway of the National Library, and the moment he arrived I leapt into his taxi and off we sped for the intown airport. Borges, a trembling leaf and utterly exhausted after a sleepless night, confessed that his greatest fear had been that he might blurt the whole thing out to Elsa at any moment. Hugo Santiago, the film-maker, who was in on the plot, and my wife were there at the flight counter with a pair of single tickets to Córdoba for Borges and me, where the lawyer had booked us into a hotel only we two knew the name of. Like good conspirators, we allowed no one knowledge of the whole plan. That way, no lies need be told, nor could anything be given away. Doña Leonor, Borges' ninety-four-year-old mother, who was punctilious in her rectitude, feared that Elsa would be quick to ring her for information, and while Leonor wanted to be able to say in truth that she did know her son's whereabouts, still she was anxious to be able to reach him if necessary. That was easy. I gave her a telephone number on a slip of paper in a sealed envelope and had her watch me secrete it in a drawer of her desk.

Bad weather delayed our flight, and a jittery Borges thought the jig was up. Santiago and I did our best to put him at ease, laughing at our own feeble attempts at gallows humour, but it was nervous laughter and both of us, I know, were quaking in our boots. Eventually, by twelve o'clock, our plane took off.

We holed up for a whole week, first in Córdoba, then in Coronel Pringles, where, after a daylong drive across the pampa, we barely arrived in time for a lecture Borges was to deliver on the subject of the Indian raids and the conquest of the desert – meaning the conquest of the Indians – of the previous century. Borges put on a brave face, stubbornly insisting that he was fit to travel these enormous distances, fit to engage in public speaking, but he was on the edge of nervous collapse. The next day his spirits picked up when he could show me the town of Coronel Suárez, some seventy-five kilometres away, named after his great-grandfather. We drove there in caravan with the mayor and other town officials of Pringles, to be met by their counterparts in Suárez, where a splendid midday banquet was laid on for us all. I sat next to the priest, a jolly fellow who, when I told him my religion was *nada*, nothing, made a rather good pun, retorting, '*Nada, nada y nunca se ahoga*' – swim, swim, and never drown. Borges, who hated puns, pronounced this one first-rate.

Eventually, we got to our destination, Pardo, where we stayed in the old dusky-rose house belonging to Bioy Casares, the one that figures in the opening of Borges' story 'The South'. Eventually, we got back to the autobiography too. In fact, by sheer coincidence, it was at Pardo that we reached the point in his life when Borges met Bioy, and we wrote those pages of the story before crackling eucalyptus fires laid on by Bioy's steward. Eventually, we finished the autobiography, not there, nor back in Buenos Aires even, but in the town of Tres Arroyos, again in the far south of the province. Borges was there to give a lecture on the poet Almafuerte. It was 29 July. In a room in the Parque Hotel, Borges lay stretched out on a single bed while I sat on the edge of the other, a cleared bedside table between us as my desk, taking down the last words of his dictation. They were not the fine words that come last in the finished essay but emendations and additions to the end of the previous paragraph, in which he speaks of longing to write, under a pen name, a merciless tirade against himself. 'Ah, the unvarnished truths I harbour!'

The next week, back home, galley proofs of *The Aleph and Other Stories* arrived; the week after, *The New Yorker*'s cable saying they were taking the autobiography as a profile. That same day, 12 August, Borges finished the last draft of his long story 'El Congreso', and together we finished the last two commentaries and our foreword to the book for Macrae. In my diary, there is no mention that the next day I posted the material off, but I must have. Instead, my mind was already on something else. The abstemious entry reads only, 'Errands for Brazil trip.' For it was just then, when he needed it, that the highly remunerative Matarazzo prize had been awarded Borges for his life's work.

'Here in Argentina,' Borges had told me on my very first morning in Buenos Aires, 'friendship is perhaps more important than love.'

BORGES ON BORGES

Jorge Luis Borges

The Royal Society of Arts, London
5 October 1983

For years I believed I had grown up in a suburb of Buenos Aires, a suburb of dangerous streets and showy sunsets. The truth is that I grew up in a garden, behind a fence of iron palings, and in a library of endless English books. I wrote that in a foreword to *Evaristo Carriego*. I still remember the illustrations of those books and most of the texts as well. They were the *Arabian Nights* in Edward William Lane's translation, the Butcher and Lang translations of *The Iliad* and *The Odyssey*, and also very lovable books such as Lewis Carroll's *Alice's Adventures in Wonderland*, *Through the Looking-Glass*, and *Sylvie and Bruno*.

Among the first things I read, I remember, were Stevenson's *New Arabian Nights*, and I remember Coleridge's 'Ancient Mariner', and then those early nightmares by H. G. Wells – *The First Men in the Moon*, *The Invisible Man*, and *The Time Machine*, which was the best of them. Kipling also came to me, not of course through his very complex stories but through the *Jungle Books* and *Kim*. But I think that I owe my greatest debt to Stevenson. I began by reading his *Treasure Island* and *Dr Jekyll and Mr Hyde*, and then I went on to other things – to those wonderful essays of his – and I keep on reading him.

I think that Stevenson invented or discovered a fairy London, as Andrew Lang said when he spoke in *Essays in Little* about Stevenson. And I think that the fairy London he discovered was the one used afterwards by Chesterton in *The Man Who Was Thursday* and *The Man Who Knew Too Much*. I mean the idea of London as a fairy city, which, amongst so many other things, perhaps it is.

I kept on reading those books, and then I discovered others. Conrad, for example, to me, *the* novelist, the outstanding novelist of all novelists. I discovered Joseph Conrad way back in 1918.

And as everybody has, I read the tales of Edgar Allan Poe. I think I should mention a special debt of gratitude to *The Narrative of Arthur Gordon Pym*. I remember quite minor books. Captain Marryat's *The Pascha of Many Tales*, *The Adventures of Mr Verdant Green*, and *Tom Brown's School Days*. Those books were given to me when I was a child or a boy.

I can remember my father's voice intoning, 'As idle as a painted ship / Upon a painted ocean'. That was one of my first memories, I think. He was always reciting Coleridge, Swinburne, Shelley, Keats, Byron, and of course Shakespeare. Poetry came to me through the English language.

At first I must have thought of language as a means of communication, but my father's intoning those verses and my hearing them – accepting them but not understanding them, perhaps – made me find out that language could also weave a spell, that language was a kind of witchcraft.

I have done most of my reading in English. When I talk of the Bible, for example, I am really talking of the King James version. This means I always thought of literature not in the realistic sense it was thought of in my country and wherever the Spanish language was spoken but rather in the way of dreams, since after all English literature is a series of splendid dreams.

I keep on being thankful to England, especially to English literature. As I have some small Latin and no Greek – no Greek at all, I am sorry to say – I think of English literature and especially of English poetry as poetry in the platonic sense. And I keep on reading the same writers I read or began reading when I was a boy. I have no memory of any time when I could not read or write. Memory is supposed to go back to when one was four years old; I must have been taught reading and writing before that, when I was three years old or so.

Philosophy also came to me through the English language. I

remember as a young man reading Bradley's *Appearance and Reality* for the first time. Much later it went into a second edition, and to my great astonishment and due amazement my name is quoted in the foreword. I also read Berkeley, of course, and Hume and William James.

Even books in other languages have come to me through English. In fact, though I have travelled all over the world, I seem never to have strayed from that library of my father's. My memory is packed full of quotations. I think reading is one of the most vivid forms of happiness.

ON WRITING IN ENGLISH

My English reading may have had some impact on my style – at least, I try to write in simple words. But I respect the English language too much to attempt writing it except now and then. I have written a few poems in it – quite bad poems, I should add. My fate is Spanish, after all, but I try not to make it into loud language but into something plain and straightforward. I would like to write in words of one syllable if I could.

ON DREAMS AND 'SHAKESPEARE'S MEMORY'

Sometimes I attain the privilege of dreaming in English. I have English dreams and Spanish dreams. I have been able to dream in no other languages. But I had a dream when I was in Michigan – a very tangled dream. And the one phrase I remembered the next morning was somebody saying to somebody else, 'I am going to sell you Shakespeare's memory – Shakespeare's personal memory.' But the word 'selling' was too commercial for me, and I changed it to I'm going to give you, or bestow on you, Shakespeare's memory. Then I wrote a long story about a German scholar being blessed, or cursed, with Shakespeare's personal memory. It was the memory Shakespeare had in 1616, a few days before his death. The hero of that story finds out first in his dreams and then in his waking life that the memories of Shakespeare have come back to him. He suddenly remembers a certain face. That face is the face of Chapman, for example, or of Ben Jonson, or of

Christopher Marlowe. He goes on until he remembers everything that Shakespeare remembered, and then he's overwhelmed and turns mad or something – I don't remember exactly. The idea is of a gift as being terrible. That's one of my most recent stories – the story of a German scholar who worships Shakespeare, as so many Germans do. I think it's quite a good story. That will be the title of the book, but I shall collect other stories. It will be my next book, to be published I suppose next year. *La memoria de Shakespeare.* I don't mean his fame but his personal memory.

ON COWARDICE
I think I'm a physical coward but not an ethical coward.

ON ETHICS
I try to be an ethical man.

ON THE WORDS 'GAUCHO' AND 'PAMPA'
I have known the gaucho more or less – through literature chiefly, of course. They are no longer to be found in the Argentine; you find them in southern Brazil or Uruguay or maybe Corrientes but not around the Province of Buenos Aires. The word 'gaucho' is never used in the country, and the word 'pampa' is utterly unknown. Except maybe through the radio, perhaps. People say '*un paesano*,' a peasant, and '*el campo*,' the country. But they never say 'gaucho' and 'pampa'. Those are literary words.

ON THE IMAGINATION
Imagination is The Thing, I should say. It's far more important than physical courage. To write you need imagination and emotion, feeling. At least, I can't write without imagination, without emotion. I have perhaps some imagination – well, a tiny amount of it. Still, most of my writing is from my reading. But Emerson said that poetry comes out of poetry.

When I write I try to be true not to things actually happening but to my particular dream at the time. I know that the reader feels it in that way. If the reader feels that a writer is lying, he lays down the book. If the reader feels that the dream is a response to a real dream then he goes on reading. That's the way I think that literature is made – by sincere dreaming. Not just juggling with words. I try to forget the words and to say what I have to say perhaps not through the words but in spite of the words, and if a book is really good you forget the words. But of course I must get the cadences. That's far more important than the plot or the metaphor or anything else – the right cadence, the right intonation for every sentence. That, I should say, is all important.

ON OLD-TIME BUENOS AIRES

The city was quite different in the old days. Patios, flat roofs, cisterns, no three-storey houses. The whole thing was different. We all knew each other. It was a very kindly city, but now it sprawls all over the province and is far too large. You can't cope with it. I'm eighty-four, and at my age one is a stranger in one's own land.

ON LIFE AT EIGHTY-FOUR

Most of my friends I have laid under ground. They have died, and I keep on stubbornly living. I don't know why, but I still keep on dreaming and weaving my dreams into books. What else can I do? I am eighty-four, I'm sorry to say; I am hopelessly blind, but I am still capable of enjoying things and of being pampered for them.

ON W. H. HUDSON

I think Hudson was a great writer but not a great storyteller or a great novelist. He was more interested in trees and birds than in men. He was a field naturalist, of course. He wrote very fine, very quiet English prose. He did that very well, but I don't think he could invent a story. He knew little about Spanish; he got all the proper names wrong and made mistakes all the time. But that is of no account. I think that I prefer his book *Idle Days in Patagonia*, for example, to when he writes about animals or birds or trees. He cared far more for them than he did for human beings or for himself.

Hudson was not a writer in the sense that Cunninghame Graham was. Cunninghame Graham could tell a story better than Hudson. Hudson had little imagination, I should say, but much feeling for things — for green things, for plants, for meadows.

ON WHAT MAKES A CLASSIC

I think the reader should enrich what he's reading. He should misunderstand the text; he should change it into something else. I suppose that when Shakespeare wrote *Macbeth* or *Hamlet* or *King Lear* those books were far simpler, but now, after Coleridge, after Bradley, after Goethe also, those books have been enriched by the generations of readers. I think that a classic is not a book written in a certain way, as Eliot thought, but rather a book read in a certain way. When you read a classic you think that everything has been thought out, that no chance words are to be found. When you read the Bible, especially, you think that the Holy Spirit has taken care of the whole thing.

Every country has its own classics, and that means that every country reads certain writers in a certain way, in a very respectful way, always trying to elicit a meaning out of every sentence, although those sentences, for all we know, may be chance sentences. So I think that a classic depends on the reader rather than on the text. In our country, I think Sarmiento's *Facundo* should have been made into a classic, but it hasn't. A classic has been made of *Martín Fierro*. That, I think, has done us no good; but still, what is there I can do about it? Nothing.

It is very strange that every country should have a celebrated classic quite unlike itself. The English go in for understatement, but I wouldn't say Shakespeare went in for understatement. He went in for metaphors, interjections, and so on. We think of the Germans as being fanatic, and yet their hero is Goethe, who was unlike most other Germans. Napoleon invaded his country, and he went to visit Napoleon. Goethe had no use for nationalism; he was untypical. The same with Cervantes. To think that Cervantes was a contemporary of the

44

Inquisition! People were strong Catholics and had a bias against the Protestants. But Cervantes was a tolerant man, a smiling man, and I suppose in his time it didn't do at all to smile in Spain. He did, and he has been chosen. Every classic is a kind of antidote against the faults of its people. That's why Shakespeare has been chosen – because he is so un-English. Goethe is so un-German; Cervantes is so un-Spanish. That's why they have been chosen, and the world has accepted them. They were all men of genius, of course.

ON THE READER'S CONTRIBUTION TO A BOOK
The reader is very important, because a book is a dead thing until it is opened and read. A book is a thing among things. When you open it and read it, if you are the right reader and its author is the right writer, then the whole thing springs into life, the book arrives, the aesthetic fact happens.

A book comes to life when it's opened and read, so that the reader contributes to the book. I think that the role of the reader is very important; he collaborates with the writer and enriches him, since he finds many things that were not intended by the writer. As does the translator, also. The translator is a very close reader; there is not much difference between translating and reading. When you translate, you have to find the meaning of every sentence, to find the right words and the right cadence, so that I think the reader is quite as important as the translator, who is a kind of reader.

Whenever I read myself I suppose I am also changing what I wrote, since I read it with different experiences. When I came back from Egypt, I read books on Egypt – Edward William Lane, for example – in a different way.

ON ROY CAMPBELL'S ST JOHN OF THE CROSS
I remember a very fine translation by a South African poet, Roy Campbell, who translated one of the finest poems in the Spanish language, that poem about '*la noche oscura del alma*' by San Juan de la Cruz. In Spanish we have, '*Estando ya mi casa sosegada*' – a rather hissing line. But Roy Campbell has translated it thus: '. . . when all my house was hushed'. It is

beautiful, really, like the music of silence. 'Hushed' is a beautiful word.

ON LEARNING LANGUAGES

I suppose hearing a language is a different way of feeling the words. I don't suppose there are synonyms really. I wonder if 'moon' means exactly the same thing as '*luna*'. I don't suppose it does; there's a slight difference. There should be – in every word. So that to learn any language is to find out different ways of viewing, of sensing the universe, the world, or ourselves. For all I know, perhaps the English Bible is superior to the Hebrew. As I have no Hebrew I can't tell, but it may be.

ON SPANISH AND ENGLISH

Spanish words are apt to be overlong. English tends to brevity. 'Ring out the old, ring in the new' – you can't say that in Spanish. Or 'dream away your life', or 'fall down and pick yourself up'. You can't pick yourself up in Spanish. The language doesn't allow it. You fall down and there you are; you can't do anything about it.

ON READING ONE'S OWN WORK

I felt an inner necessity to write; I had to do it. I didn't want to publish, but one way to be rid of something you have written is to publish it. I suppose I should have gone on reading and not writing. I apologize. I don't like my own stuff. I prefer what other people write to what I write.

If an author reads his own work he knows all about the rough drafts that came before the printed work, so he can't properly enjoy it. But if you read somebody else's writings you know nothing of the rough drafts and you can enjoy the whole thing, you can take it for granted. But an author knows only too well what he meant to do, what he did, what he failed to do. He finds out that this adjective is wrong, that things can be changed. When he reads something by somebody else he accepts it and reads it in a thankful way, in a respectful way. But I can hardly read what I write respectfully or thankfully. I have to put up with it.

ON WALTER SCOTT
I was bored stiff by him, I am sorry to say; I am utterly
unworthy of Sir Walter. Dunbar is the finest Scottish poet.

ON 'THE ALEPH'
I began with an abstract idea and thought of eternity. In
eternity you have all moments of time, past and to come,
packed into a single divine moment – eternity, or as Wilkins
called it, 'everness'. That's a far better word.

Then I said I would take this abstract idea of eternity –
perhaps impossible, perhaps something that had never happened – and apply it to another category. Since in eternity you
have all our yesterdays, as Shakespeare said, the present, and
all our future days and the future days of mankind, packed into
a single moment, why not suppose a single point in space
wherein the whole of space can be found. The story began with
that abstract idea of a spot in space comprising all space, and
that was taken from the idea of a moment in time implying all
time.

The rest of the story was made up of jokes about my friends
and about myself, and then the whole was ringed in by common things. The rest was given me afterwards – we have
irony and humour perhaps not to be found in my other stories.

ON 'THE INTRUDER'
It was a brutal story, I'm sorry to say, but it was meant to be
brutal. It shows the contempt men have for women in my
country and in South America generally. It's a story about
machismo, which I thoroughly dislike. It's a very simple story,
but I didn't know how to end it. I was dictating it to my mother
(I was already blind) and I came to the point where the elder
brother has to tell the younger that he has killed the girl. And
then I said to my mother, 'The fate of the story depends on the
words he says. Try and help me.' She was taking down the
story, she didn't like it, and she said, 'Let me think.' And then
she said in a quite different voice, 'I know what he said.' It was
as if he had actually said it, but of course it was merely fiction.
And then I said, 'Well, write it down.' And then she wrote

down, '*A trabajar, hermano. Esta mañana la maté.* To work, brother, this morning I killed her.' She found the right words, but she didn't like the story; however, at that moment she believed in the story. And then she made me promise never to write about people like that again; she found them utterly uninteresting and repugnant. 'Don't keep on writing about knives and knife duels,' she said; 'I'm sick and tired of it all.'

She had found her way inside the story and I hadn't really. She knew far better about the story than I did, since she found the right words and the right intonation and the right cadence to the words.

ON READING HISTORIANS

I have spent my life reading and rereading Gibbon's *Decline and Fall.* A wonderful book, I should say. And also an epic book by Voltaire on Charles XII of Sweden, the *Histoire de Charles XII.* Voltaire began by mocking him and then he saw the whole thing as an epic. A very interesting recent book is Liddell Hart's book on the real war, the First World War.

I have read Prescott. I think the first book on history I ever read was Prescott's *Conquest of Peru* and later I went on to the *Conquest of Mexico.* I must have been a child at the time. I was greatly interested by them. Of course, they were written in a romantic way; you can't think of them in connection with Gibbon. Gibbon was a very intelligent man; Prescott perhaps wasn't.

ON READING THE BRITANNICA

I am very fond of encyclopaedias. Encyclopaedias are meant for idle and curious men, and I am idle and curious, so encyclopaedias seem to be the right stuff for me. The old editions of the Britannica were meant for reading, not for reference. I have the 1911 edition; therein you find articles by Edmund Gosse, an article by Stevenson, articles by Macaulay – the article on Dr Johnson, for example – an article by Giles on the history of Chinese literature. Those books were meant for reading purposes, not reference purposes.

ON BEING LATIN-AMERICAN

I wonder if there is such a thing as Latin America. I don't think of myself as Latin American; I think of myself as Argentine or Uruguayan, perhaps, but certainly not a Peruvian or a Colombian or a Mexican.

ON THE PAMPAS INDIANS

Peru and Mexico had cultures of their own, but in my country the Indians just roamed about and were barbarians – fine riders, fine fighters, but quite unimaginative. They had no mythology of their own, only a few superstitions.

My English grandmother lived in Junín, on the border, from 1870 to 1874. She had met many Indian caciques. They had never seen a house in their lives, because they lived in tents. So to them such commonplace things as a door, a window, a patio, a cistern, a flat roof, walls, houses were quite new, and they showed no astonishment. Perhaps those things were too new to be wondered at. I think it was that; I don't think the Indians were stupid. I think those things were beyond their ken, so that they couldn't even be amazed by them. They were silent people, very stubborn, very brave. They were better riders than the gauchos. They never used spurs or bridles. They rode bareback, and they could be wounded and never speak out. They could die in silence; they could suffer great physical pain and never complain. They roamed all over the country – all over the pampas, to use a word I don't suppose they had ever heard in their lives. They could be very cruel also.

What is called in the States 'the winning of the west' is called in my country 'la conquista del desierto'. It was very ruthless, because when the white men won they cut the throats of the Indians, when the Indians won they speared the white men. It took the white men years to do it. They had firearms and the Indians had only spears and knives, so of course the Indians were defeated. They were doomed to defeat. What could they do against a man with a rifle? Nothing at all. My grandfather, Colonel Borges, fought in that particular war of conquest.

ON THE FRENCH INFLUENCE IN SPANISH-AMERICAN LITERATURE

French influence was very strong on Spanish-American writers, because they thought of literature in terms of three writers – Hugo, Verlaine, and Edgar Allan Poe. Poe came to them through the French versions of Baudelaire and Mallarmé. I wonder if Darío had English; I don't think he had. I don't think Lugones had English, but they all knew French; they all could enjoy French literature. It's very strange, but the French influence was stronger on us than the Spanish. Spanish-American writers all thought of literature in terms of French literature. Of course, that also gave us Shakespeare, since Hugo had written a very fine book on Shakespeare.

ON POE

I think of Poe more as an English writer than as an American writer. At least, he never tried to be an American – unlike Walt Whitman. I don't think Poe had any use for that kind of thing. He was merely dreaming away and leaving us wonderful dreams. He invented the detective story and he had so many illustrious followers – Chesterton, perhaps, was the most important of them. But they were all begotten by Edgar Allan Poe.

ON BYRON

In the case of Byron, you think less of what he wrote than of the man himself. He had his own image, and that was his real work – the image of Lord Byron – to be worshipped all over the world. And yet 'Don Juan' is a very fine poem. He's best, I should say, at trick rhymes at the end of every stanza.

ON THE TANGO

The tango evolved in the bawdy houses. That was in 1880, and the instruments were not folk instruments – not popular – they were the violin, flute, and piano. It began in Rosario, in Buenos Aires, and in Montevideo. Nobody knows exactly where, but it was not popular. It came from the bawdy houses, from the pimps, from the young men about town, and from the women, of course. I think at the time those women were Polish. The tango was not accepted by the people until the aristocracy took it up. When the people knew that it was being danced in Paris, that lent an air of respectability to it, since Paris was a kind of national superstition.

The tango is rather old-fashioned nowadays. It's no longer popular amongst young people. They go in for rock and roll.

ON FILMING BORGES STORIES
The director should stray from the text and invent as much as possible. That's his bounden duty – to be unfaithful to the text.

ON BEING TAUGHT BERKELEY'S PHILOSOPHY
My father taught me philosophy in his own way. With the aid of chessmen and a chessboard he taught me about the paradoxes of Zeno. I remember he asked me, 'What's the colour of an orange?' I said that the orange was orange-coloured – between red and yellow. He didn't answer, but then went on to say, 'What's the shape of the orange?' I said it was round. 'Yes, but what does that mean?'

'Well,' I said, 'I feel it all around.' Then he said, 'That's what comes afterwards.' He would take up the orange and say, 'Do you think the orange tastes the savour of orange all the time?'

'No, of course it doesn't,' I said.

'Well, what is the orange besides being round, and yellow, and having that peculiar taste?' He was teaching me Berkeley's philosophy without mentioning Berkeley. That was the right way to set about it, I think. He taught me philosophy with no proper names, with no historic sense at all. He gave me – I must have been twelve at the time – a biographical history of philosophy, and therein I found out that all those jokes of my father's were main questions of philosophy.

ON THE HOLY TRINITY
My father once said to me, 'The world is so strange that anything is possible – even the Holy Trinity.'

LATIN AMERICA AND OTHER QUESTIONS

Graham Greene

The Royal Society of Arts, London
1 October 1984

I would like to recount the occasion on which I met Borges. I was invited with him to lunch by Victoria Ocampo, and I was dispatched to the National Library to lead him to her flat. Almost as soon as the door had shut behind us at the National Library, we began to talk about literature. Borges talked about the influence G. K. Chesterton had had on him and the influence Robert Louis Stevenson had had on his later stories. He spoke of the prose of Stevenson as a great influence. I then interjected a remark. Robert Louis Stevenson did write one good poem. A poem about his ancestors. His ancestors had built the great lighthouses on the coast of Scotland, and I knew that ancestors were an interest of Borges'. The poem began,

> Say not of me that weakly I declined
> The labours of my sires, and fled the sea,
> The towers we founded and the lamps we lit,
> To play at home with paper like a child.

It was a very noisy, crowded Buenos Aires street. Borges stopped on the edge of the pavement and recited the whole poem to me, word perfect. After an agreeable lunch, he sat on a sofa and quoted large chunks of Anglo-Saxon. That, I'm afraid, I was not able to follow. But I looked at his eyes as he recited and I was amazed at the expression in those blind eyes. They did not look blind at all. They looked as if they were looking into themselves in some curious way, and they had great nobility.

Borges too, of course, had this feeling for ancestors, for the gauchos of the past. His later tales are full of stories of the gauchos, and in one of them he wrote, 'Just as men of certain countries worship and feel the call of the sea, we Argentines in turn yearn for the boundless plains that ring under a horse's hooves.'

He was a man of great courage. At one time, during the second period of Perón, when he was living with his old mother, there was a mysterious phone call. A male voice said, 'We're coming to kill you and your mother.' Borges' mother replied, 'I'm ninety years old, so you'd better come quickly. And as for my son, it will be easy for you, since he is blind.' This, I think, gives a picture of what the family was like.

To me, Borges speaks for all writers. Over and over again in his books, I find phrases which are my experience as a writer. He calls writing 'a guided dream', and on one occasion he wrote,

> I do not write for a select minority, which means nothing to me, nor for that adulated platonic entity known as 'The Masses.' Both abstractions, so dear to the demagogue, I disbelieve in. I write for myself and for my friends, and I write to ease the passing of time.

That, I think, will make every writer feel close to him.

I don't remember where Victoria Ocampo and I first met. I think it was in Europe. She invited me to stay with her in Argentina, and we went down in those cold summers of Argentina – so-called summers – to Mar del Plata to her house there, which had no heating, and we sat talking for hours in front of a little electric fire. After that, I always saw her as I passed through Argentina. In 1972, for example, I stayed with her on my way to Chile to see President Allende. I stayed with her on my way to Paraguay when I went up the Paraná River by boat.

We had a regular routine of going to the cinema. She loved the cinema. Even the worst film in some out-of-the-way cinema pleased her. I was very fond of her; she helped a great deal by reading the translations of my books and criticizing them. She herself translated one of my plays, and I got to know her past extraordinary life, which one is not at liberty to talk about.

I have read García Márquez and I have a great respect for his work. I cannot say *One Hundred Years of Solitude* is a book I enjoyed. It was to me rather in the same category as *Ulysses*, a book that I profoundly respect but haven't enjoyed. On the other hand, I've enjoyed the company of García Márquez. We have seen quite a bit of each other in Panama.

I'm not very well up in Latin-American literature. Borges I've read and Sábato, another Argentine, who is also a friend, but I'm not very well versed in any others.

I feel very strongly that Argentina is a tragic place. I feel that the Falklands War was a tragedy and it was almost an incestuous war. One thinks of the close ties that have existed between England and Argentina before the days of Videla.

Pablo Neruda, the poet, who was ambassador in Paris at the time, gave me an invitation to go to Chile, and I went in 1972. I had two encounters with Allende. He was very kind to me. He greeted me on my arrival, and I had one prolonged lunch with him. He had most of his ministers with him, and I was struck by the frankness of his replies to questions.

I have always felt that his death, in its way, was just as romantic as Che Guevara's. Che Guevara's was in the more obvious Byronic mode. But for this small plump doctor, with his liking for women, very moderate in politics, to die with a gun in his hand and a steel helmet on his head, seems to me more romantic than Che Guevara's death.

Omar Torrijos invited me to Panama four years running, and I would have gone a fifth year, only his death came about.

I suddenly got a telegram from one of his counsellors inviting me on his behalf to go to Panama. I didn't know why. But by the end of the first visit we were good friends. Then I went back the following year, in 1977, and became one of the Panamanian delegation to the signing to the treaty, which was a sort of joke of Torrijos', but it was interesting for once to see all these dictators lined up on the platform. Torrijos had not wished them invited; he had wanted Carter to invite only Venezuela, Colombia, and Peru, who had aided him. He hadn't wished to have Videla of Argentina, and Banzer of Bolivia, and Pinochet of Chile. He hadn't wished them there. Carter had insisted on having them all. And for me it was very interesting to see the whole bunch of them.

To ask if we can learn anything from Latin America is rather like asking what we can learn from *King Lear*, the tragedies of Shakespeare. I'm thinking of the tragic situation of Central America. It's difficult to say what we learn from it, but we must be learning something and it must be appealing to the imagination. Such things as the murder of Archbishop Romero, for example. Thank God we are not in danger of going that way ourselves, but I suppose we must somehow be learning something in our unconscious.

Which authors most influenced you to become a writer?
I would say in my very early days I was inspired by writers who are now almost forgotten: Henty, Captain Brereton, Percy Westerman, Marjorie Bowen. They gave me the desire to write stories rather than experimental novels.

Later, when I really began writing, I was badly under the influence of Conrad. I said badly because I was under the influence of what I consider his one bad book, *The Arrow of Gold*. That's the book where he himself was under the influence of Henry James. Henry James too was an influence, technically, in my work. From him I learnt the importance of a point of view. But Stevenson, who was a cousin of my mother's, has also influenced me as a storyteller.

Which character out of your novels have you liked the best and which has frightened you most?
I don't think I have been frightened by any of my characters, having created them myself I feel safe – but I suppose otherwise I would say perhaps Pinkie in *Brighton Rock* was the most frightening.

I like the character of Charley Fortnum in *The Honorary Consul* as much as any, and I like that book better than *The Power and the Glory*, because in *The Power and the Glory* the characters remain the same all the way through. The priest is the same priest at the end that he is at the beginning; the lieutenant of police is the same as he was at the beginning. Whilst in *The Honorary Consul* I think I did something which was more difficult: the characters changed. The doctor was not the same as he was at the start and the Honorary Consul was not the same.

How did you come to be known as a Catholic writer?
Nobody knew that I was a Catholic writer for a good many years. I became a Catholic in 1927; my first book was published in 1929. Nobody discovered I was a Catholic until 1938, when *Brighton Rock* was published, and then I became dubbed a Catholic writer. I resent the phrase. I say that I am a writer who happens to be a Catholic, because I do not consider myself altogether an orthodox Catholic and I do not wish to be constricted in my characters or in their motives as I am afraid Mauriac was a bit constricted by his Church.

How do you define your political position?
I would say that from the start of my writing, in a book called *It's a Battlefield*, my political opinions became obvious. They were obviously to the left. If it hadn't become a dirty word, I would call myself a social democrat, but certainly I am on the left. I don't like to be called anti-American. I have been very critical in *The Quiet American* and elsewhere of American foreign policy. American foreign policy is not American individuals, and I have been critical of the consumer society – the exaggeration of the consumer society. Again, that does not mean that one is anti-Americans.

Have you ever been tempted to write verse?
Poetry has been very important to me, especially Browning. My own verse has not been important to me, because it is not good enough. I have occasionally indulged in verse. For

example, I wrote a ballade on the wedding of Princess Grace of Monaco. I think I can still remember the envoi:

> Prince, you may draw the curtains close
> And set a sentry on the stair,
> Then lie down by the bride you chose,
> But Father Tucker will be there.

Is it essential that a novel be enjoyed?
I am not sure. There may be a certain masochism in the reader.

Which of your women characters have you liked the most?
I think people will disagree with me, but I think possibly the character in *The End of the Affair*. I did receive a compliment from Theodora Benson, who was a woman writer and a contemporary of mine. She wrote to me and said that the journal had not been written by me but by a woman, who had helped me. I took that as a great compliment.

Which particular British novelists writing now do you most admire?
I would like to group two or three together. I am not sure which of them I like best. William Trevor, Brian Moore, Muriel Spark, Beryl Bainbridge. I like that group of writers.

How did the Anglo-Texan Society come about?
It came about under the influence of Black Velvet. A friend of mine, John Sutro, and I had gone to Edinburgh to see Trevor Howard in a play, and we met two charming Texan girls and took them to the theatre and the next day, going back on the train, John Sutro said, 'We have done ourselves well at lunch. Let's found an Anglo-Texan Society.' So I wrote a letter to *The Times* speaking of a special cultural and historic relationship. I signed it as president and Sutro as secretary. I left the next day for Kenya and the Mau Mau rebellion, and when I got to Nairobi I found a telegram from John Sutro saying fifty applicants on the first day, including Sir Hartley Shawcross

and Samuel Guinness, the banker. It then dragged its slow length along for some years, and I believe it is still in existence. I made the excuse of resigning. I cannot remember now what my excuse was. It was some difference of opinion over American foreign policy, and I resigned from the presidency. A politician became president in my place. I think the society is still going.

How satisfied have you been with the translation of your novels into film?
I did *The Third Man* myself and I think it is a good film. I did *The Fallen Idol* myself and I think it is a good film. I did *The Comedians* myself and I think it is not a good film. I did *Our Man in Havana* and I think it is not bad as a film. Some of the great film makers, like Cukor and Fritz Lang and Mancovitz, have made intolerably bad films out of my books, and I would say that there are only about half a dozen reasonably good ones out of some twenty-five or so.

What inspired you to write Monsignor Quixote?
I was in the habit of travelling in Spain with a Spanish priest who was a professor of English literature at Madrid, and I think the idea came to me one night in Évora, in Portugal, when he and I and an ex-student of his, who had lent his car and acted as driver, had drunk two bottles of vinho verde and we then had a half bottle to follow. I said this was a good illustration of a Trinity: born in the same year, same substance, and perhaps the half bottle was the Holy Ghost to add a little bit of pep to the whole thing. The next day Father Durán was very remorseful, because he said it should have been three whole bottles. So we went back that night and made it theologically correct, and it was then that the idea came to me.

What is the least favourite of your books?
The book that I like least – but you won't be able to buy it, because it will never be republished – is *Rumour at Nightfall*, which was about the Carlist wars in Spain. It was a very bad

book and very much under the influence of Conrad. After that I gave up reading Conrad for thirty years.

Would you say that Conrad's influence on you was good or bad?
I had been under the influence of his one bad book, *The Arrow of Gold*. There were too many metaphors, too many similes, too many adjectives, too many attempts at poetic writing. Poetic prose is horrible. I think one should either write poetry or prose, and for that reason I didn't read Conrad again for many years. My eyes were opened by an unfriendly review by Mr Swinnerton, which was absolutely correct, and I have every reason to be grateful to him, because it opened my eyes to where I was going. I only felt brave enough to read Conrad again in 1959, when I went to stay in a leper colony in the Congo. Then I dared to do it; I felt I had got my own style by this time and I wasn't in danger.

Has Nostromo *affected you at all, particularly in your perception of inter-American politics?*
Curiously enough, I have always found *Nostromo* difficult to read. I read it fairly recently – perhaps ten years ago – and still found it difficult. I'm not saying it's a bad book, like *The Arrow of Gold*, but I have always found it for some reason difficult. It doesn't hold me like his other books do.

Did you have any living person in mind when you drew the character of the priest in The Power and the Glory?
I got the idea for him in Villahermosa from a Scottish doctor who had lived all his life in Tabasco. He told me about a priest who was so drunk he had baptised the doctor's son with a girl's name. The priest had disappeared in the persecution. In Tabasco, even when I went there in the winter of 1937, there was only the back wall of the cathedral standing in Villahermosa. There were no churches left, and a woman said to me that they smuggled the priest in to a baptism every now and then from Mexico City. In Mexico City, everything seemed normal, because that's the place where the tourists went. This gave me the idea for the book.

What was your impression of the political regime in Mexico in those years?
I didn't like the political regime then and I've never been happy with the Mexican revolution. It has always seemed to me a phony revolution. They were very proud of themselves after Castro came to power in Cuba in allowing Cubana Airlines to fly to and from Mexico City against the American blockade. But I travelled to Havana in 1961 from Mexico City. I couldn't get a visa to return. I had a visa for entering, but I couldn't get a visa to return by the same route. Before getting on the plane and passing through immigration, one's photograph was taken and sent to the FBI. It didn't seem to me to be what I would have called a left-wing revolution, and when I came back I had great difficulty in getting a visa to return from Cuba to Mexico City for four days. When I arrived at the airport somebody from the British embassy was there in case I had difficulty, and I was kept waiting for two and a half hours. There were only thirty people on the plane and I was kept waiting all that time having my luggage searched. So I have never really believed in the Mexican revolution.

What are your views now on the dangerous travels through Africa that resulted in your book Journey Without Maps?
I don't think it was dangerous except from a point of view of health. One had a very friendly reception in the hinterland of Liberia and a hut would always be swept out for one to sleep in and food was obtainable. From the health point of view it was a bit dangerous, but I was very grateful for that journey; it gave me a certain love of Africa, although it meant that I had to go back to Sierra Leone during the war, because they needed someone who knew that part of the world. It was not so pleasant living there as spending three months there.

After having moved around the world so much how did you come to live in Antibes?
I got to know Antibes first around 1948. I used to go down to join Alexander Korda, who had a boat there, and we used to go off together. So that I got to know the town and I liked the

town because it's got great character. The old town still remains, the ramparts remain, the Fort Carré remains. It's the one town on the coast where I find it easy to live. I like the Antibois people. Later I went to live there. I had always planned in a way to end my days in France because of the good food and the good wine and the good bread. The bread isn't what it was, but the wine is.

Why haven't more of your books been made into films?
Practically every one has. Except the one which was written definitely scenically, not that the intention was for becoming a film; it was under the influence of films: *It's a Battlefield*. It's the one that's never been made into a film. But I think all the others have been, for better or worse, generally for worse. I think the novel is not a good route for a film, because you have to cut a novel so much, and you may think that you are cutting something completely unimportant, somebody's taste for orange juice or God knows what, and when you've cut that the character has changed, you've lost the dimension. Cutting is an absolute essential for the novel; I think the short story makes far better film.

What is it that has drawn you to Spain and Latin America?
I really don't know. It's a mystery to me. Before I had had a book published at all I wrote two books which were never published. One of them dealt with Spanish refugees in London at the time of the Carlist wars. I then wrote a book which I won't see published again. It was a very bad book, called *Rumour at Nightfall*, which took place in Spain. I then went to Mexico years later to write a book on the religious persecution, not a novel but a non-fiction book, and I don't now know what has always drawn me towards Spain and Latin America. Of recent years I have become very fond of Panama, because I was invited four years running by Omar Torrijos and became very fond of him and made great friends there. It's a mystery for me too why I got so mixed up with Latin America.

THE FOUNDATIONS
OF A FRIENDSHIP

H. S. Ferns

The Royal Society of Arts, London
30 October 1985

In 1918, in his seventy-seventh year, W. H. Hudson published an account of his childhood in Argentina, *Far Away and Long Ago*. It is, perhaps, the finest book in English about the pampa, that great treasure house of nature, which has sustained and enriched the Argentine community for three centuries or more. From his birth in 1841, on the ranch *Los Veinte-cinco Ombues*, named for a row of twenty-five ombú trees that sprouted there, until he contracted typhus fever during a visit to Buenos Aires in 1856, Hudson grew and happily flourished in a free and intimate friendship with the animals, wild and domestic, the plants and flowers, the birds and reptiles, and the people of the plains – his family, their neighbours, and the wanderers over the vast expanse of Buenos Aires province. In his fifteenth year, Hudson visited Buenos Aires. The pestilence in the city brought him close to death, and, as he left his boyhood behind, he experienced what he described as the dark night of the soul. But until the very end of his life there remained with him at the centre of his being a memory of the freedom, beauty, and natural abundance that he had known as a boy under the immense pale blue sky of the pampa, where pure white clouds floated softly, it seemed, for ever.

Like Hudson, I want to remember and perhaps explain something which is far away and long ago but which, like his memory of the pampa, is still present as an unforgettable part of human experience – that is to say, the friendship between Britain and Argentina that flourished in the nineteenth century and for part of our own.

The circumstances in which relations were first established between the British and the community now called Argentina

67

held anything but the promise of friendship. The invasion of the Viceroyalty of the Río de la Plata in 1806, and the seizure and occupation of its capital city, Buenos Aires, by British forces under the command of Sir Home Popham were not events which one might suppose could lead to friendship, cooperation, and understanding. The fact that Popham's action owed nothing to the initiative of the British Government provided no mitigating excuse, because the popularity in Britain of his initial success induced the Government to mount a second, formidable, and official invasion, which failed even more miserably than the unofficial act and for which, according to Sir John Fortescue, the British army historian, Popham deserved to be hanged by the citizens of Buenos Aires.

This bad beginning had within it something miraculous. Against all ordinary expectations it was a creative event for both victor and vanquished. The people of the River Plate discovered that with little or no assistance from the Spanish Crown they had created the means of protecting themselves. The invaders likewise made a discovery – that a connection with the people of the Río de la Plata was worth having and that violent military action was not the means of bringing this about.

The conflict of 1806–07 was the real beginning of the Argentine Republic, not because it immediately ended Spanish sovereignty in the Río de la Plata but because it demonstrated both to the people of Buenos Aires and to the British Government that the political initiative had passed from Spain, that the colony in the Río de la Plata had ceased to be a dependency, and that, though inchoate as a state, this colony had become an autonomous force on the international political stage.

Ironically, the British Government began to recognize this fact before the capitulation of their expeditionary force to the army of Santiago de Liniers. In March 1807, the Government which had despatched the expedition to the River Plate was replaced by one led by the Duke of Portland, in which Viscount Castlereagh was the Secretary of State for War. In a memorandum dated 1 May 1807, Castlereagh questioned the wisdom of what was being attempted in the River Plate. It was a mistake, he argued, to scatter the comparatively small British army around the world at a time when Britain was at war with Napoleon Bonaparte. Defeating Napoleon and re-establishing free intercourse with the continent of Europe was Britain's principal interest. Referring to the force under General Whitelocke, Castlereagh declared that he 'certainly [did] entertain a very *strong persuasion* that the policy upon which we are now acting [in the River Plate] will be productive of little commercial or political benefit, and must be a great waste of our military resources.' British action did not involve the liberation of the people there; it was making them into enemies. 'It is not', Castlereagh maintained, 'wonderful that the people of all classes [in the River Plate] should look with great jealousy to the circumstances under which we come amongst them. . . .' The British Government would have to discover 'whether some principle of acting more consonant to the sentiments and interest of the people of South America cannot be taken up . . . which may relieve us from the hopeless task of conquering this extensive country, against the temper of its population.' Within a few weeks, the capitulation of General Whitelocke demonstrated the hopelessness emphasized by Castlereagh.

Castlereagh went on to argue that, although Britain ought not to encourage a revolution against the Spanish Crown in South America, such a course would be justified if Napoleon gained control in Spain. If liberation from European control became necessary, then 'in looking to any scheme of liberating South America, it seems indefensible that we should not present ourselves in any other light than as auxiliaries and protectors.'

Castlereagh's objective realism and an acceptance of the fact that military conquest did not work became the foundation of British policy vis-à-vis Latin America. On the Argentine side, a matching realism emerged as the revolution against Spain advanced towards the goal of political independence. It became the conviction of the dominant ranching interests that the community of the River Plate required, first, access to wider markets for the produce of the country than could be provided by the restrictive monopoly of trade in the hands of Spanish commercial interests and, second, the free admission of more people, goods, and capital resources than hitherto.

Given these two interdependent views of public policy, it became possible to construct a legal framework for Anglo-Argentine relations. This was provided by the treaty of friendship and navigation between the United Kingdom of Great Britain and the United Provinces of the Río de la Plata signed in February 1825, and ratified in London in May of that year. It is necessary to emphasize that this was a formal legal document to which both parties attached the greatest importance and which bound the hands of the parties in their relations with each other.

The treaty, a well-matured example of the 'new liberalism' in international political and commercial relations, was very different from the treaties governing trade and political intercourse negotiated in the age of mercantilism, which by the 1820s was in terminal decline. How different it was, for example, from the treaty which fixed the relations between Britain and Brazil, negotiated between the British and the Portuguese Crown in 1807 and maintained after Brazilian independence until 1843. That treaty, negotiated from a position of strength by the British, guaranteed a preferential, unalterable tariff on British imports into Brazilian markets but left British markets closed to Brazilian products, permitting only their re-export from Britain. Furthermore, it provided a special status for British subjects resident in Brazil, who, under the treaty, enjoyed access to a special court established to deal with British conflicts of interest with Brazilians and among British subjects.

Nothing of this kind appeared in the Anglo-Argentine treaty. The terms were reciprocal and equal for both parties. The sovereign power of neither government was impaired. The laws of the United Provinces of the Río de la Plata applied equally to all residents, as British law did in Britain. Neither British subjects nor British products enjoyed a privileged position in Argentina, nor did Argentines and their products in Britain. Both powers agreed to treat each other on a 'most favoured nation' basis – that is, no foreign subjects or products entering the jurisdiction of each power would be treated better than the Britons and Argentines were treated in each other's territories. The legislative autonomy of each party to the treaty was acknowledged. When, in 1837, the government of General Juan Manuel de Rosas raised tariffs on foreign imports for a second time, Palmerston told the British Minister in Buenos Aires that he did not 'claim the right to remonstrate formally', but he wished him to argue with the authorities in Buenos Aires about the virtues of free trade. The treaty allowed the British Government to talk but not to act, and this was an accepted fact.

In negotiating the treaty there were, however, two topics – religious freedom and immunity from conscription for military service – which concerned the British authorities and prompted them to establish a legal foundation for the protection of British subjects in the River Plate. It was easy enough for Britain to concede reciprocity in these subjects because military conscription had never existed in Britain, and in practical terms no Argentine in Britain was likely to be affected by the existing laws governing the established churches there. It was otherwise in Argentina. There the population was overwhelmingly Roman Catholic, and military conscription was a practice which the government employed in a variety of ways.

As a result of the revolution in the River Plate, church and state had been separated and the Inquisition had been abolished, but the Roman Catholic Church had considerable power expressed in laws affecting marriage and public worship, and this power was reinforced by widespread popular support. The British Consul General Woodbine Parish, who negotiated the treaty, was aware of the problems even though those with whom he was negotiating were professedly liberals. It was conceded by the Argentine negotiators that religious freedom for Protestants ought to be granted and protected by law.

This was done. It was soon recognized by the official representatives of the British Government in the River Plate that the guarantee of religious freedom in the treaty ought not to be converted into a licence to engage in Protestant missionary activity in Argentina, and that its provisions did not constitute a privilege enabling British subjects to break the law on the subject, for example, of mixed marriages. When a wealthy British merchant defied the law by marrying a Catholic woman without the consent of either her father or the church, the British Minister in Buenos Aires refused to protest against the annulment of the marriage, the imprisonment of the bride in a convent, and the banishment of her suitor. When indignant British residents presented a strong protest to the British Minister, he told them that they could not regard themselves 'a separate community exempt as British subjects from the operation of the law of the land and enjoying rights distinct from those of the Citizens of the Republick'. Then he added by way of clarification that he did not take instruction from the British residents in Argentina but from His Majesty's Government. The British Government supported him, and so did the law officers of the Crown.

In any political community there are always individuals and groups seeking to influence the policies of their government in order to serve their own interests, whether economic, religious, or ideological. Peace and friendship between nation states depends upon the extent to which governments can harmonize or contain the demands of their citizens so that peace and friendship can be maintained. It is a melancholy fact of life that governments sometimes fail in their endeavours, even abandoning their attempts, and end up trying to solve relations between states by the use of the powers at their disposal for the purpose of imposing one-sided solutions.

Keeping this generalization in mind, let us now examine briefly the records of the British and Argentine authorities in preserving the peace and friendship that can be observed as a feature of Anglo-Argentine intercourse during the century following the first treaty of friendship and navigation. (The word 'first' is introduced advisedly, because in 1849 a new treaty of friendship and navigation was negotiated to take the place of that of 1825, which had broken down as a result of political differences involving the use of force by the British Government.) Soon after the ratification of that first treaty two issues emerged which were likely to cause trouble. One concerned money and the other territory.

An immediate development following the signing of the treaty was the flotation of an Argentine bond issue in the London money market, handled by Baring Brothers and Company. By the standards of the time this involved a comparatively large sum of money, £1,000,000, which, taking account of the issue price and the bankers' charges, netted the Argentine authorities a cash sum of approximately £550,000. From the first receipt of the proceeds of the loan, its interest and sinking fund charges were in default. The bondholders soon organized themselves into a pressure group in Britain. What was the British Government to do? When a committee of the bondholders wrote to Lord Palmerston, the Foreign Secretary, on the subject of their claims, he instructed his undersecretary 'to inform [them] that the grievance of which [they] complain arising as it does out of a private speculation of a purely private nature, His Majesty's Government cannot properly make any official application to the Government of Buenos Aires.'

This was and remained the British Government's policy. They would make sympathetic noises to disappointed creditors and they were willing to suggest to the Argentines that they ought to pay, but Britain was never prepared to *do* anything or threaten anyone on behalf of investors in Argentine funds. The Argentines, particularly General Rosas, who dominated Argentine political life from 1828 to 1852, always acknowledged that the Argentines owed the bondholders money, and sometimes he paid them small sums on account, but the local demands on the very limited resources of the government in Buenos Aires always had a priority, which left the bondholders with little and sometimes nothing at all.

The other issue was territory – namely, the Falkland Islands. Argentina claimed the islands as a successor state of Spain. The British claimed them on the strength of agreements they had made with the Spanish government. Both the British and the

Spaniards had planted a small settlement in the islands in the late eighteenth century, but neither settlement had proved permanent. Until the mid-1820s, the islands were in the possession of no power and were visited only by whaling or sealing ships or other vessels seeking fresh water or the opportunity to rest their crews and hunt wild cattle for food. When the Argentines were planning to establish their authority in the islands, the British warned them that these were British possessions. No notice was taken of these warnings. The first Argentine settlement was destroyed and dispersed by the United States Navy on orders from the United States consul in Buenos Aires, who held that the Argentine governor was a pirate interfering with American sealing and whaling vessels. When the Argentines attempted to re-establish their authority, the British stepped in and the Argentines were asked to leave. They did so protesting that they were yielding to superior force. They denounced the British occupation and never acknowledged its legality, nor were they ever to do anything that might implicitly admit the claim of the British Crown to sovereignty in the islands.

General Rosas took a practical view of the Falkland/Malvinas problem. In 1841, he instructed the Argentine Minister in London to explore the possibility of exchanging clear title to the Falkland Islands for a cancellation of the debt remaining on account of the loan of 1824. There was no response whatever in Britain to the Argentine overture. Among the many mistakes made by Lord Aberdeen in dealing with Argentina, this was the worst. Never has the parsimony and lack of imagination of a politician been so visited onto the children of the third, fourth, and fifth generation. And perhaps beyond.

At the time, however, Lord Aberdeen's other mistakes were serious enough – so much so that they came close to destroying all semblance of good relations between the two nations. Mistakes, of course, are mistakes, and Lord Aberdeen and his advisers in the Foreign Office can be accounted muddle-headed, but this is an insufficient explanation of the Anglo-French intervention in the River Plate between 1842 and 1847, which resulted in the seizure of the island of Martín García, the seizure of Argentine ships of war, and the forcible entry of the rivers Uruguay and Paraguay by British naval vessels.

It is not easy to explain in a few words what went wrong between Britain and Argentina during those five years between 1842 and 1847. There is no evidence that Lord Aberdeen consciously and deliberately changed British policy in relation to Argentina or that he planned to dictate by force to the government of General Rosas. On the other hand, Aberdeen yielded, or seemed to yield, to a variety of pressures upon his government to open up trade opportunities in the River Plate and to bring to an end the political disorders which interfered with British commerce, particularly in Uruguay. The cumulative effect of imprecision of policy in London and personal initiatives by British diplomatic and military agents in the River Plate was a dangerous inconsistency of action, which imperilled not only the interests but the lives of British residents in Argentina.

Given that the Anglo-French intervention in the River Plate involved the blockade of Buenos Aires, the landing of British troops in Montevideo, and the use of force by the Royal Navy to effect the passage of ships up and down the rivers Uruguay and Paraguay, it is a miracle that a full-scale war between Britain and Argentina did not break out. That it did not owed much to General Rosas' subtlety and rational understanding of the self-interest of his people and to his imaginative grasp of the real interests of Britain. At the height of the crisis he made it plain to the British Minister in Buenos Aires that he knew that by the use of force the British and the French could capture Buenos Aires, but he wanted them to know that they could never conquer Argentina and that armed force could not protect the lives of Europeans resident there. He assumed that the British, knowing these facts, would come to their senses and restore the good order necessary for fruitful intercourse between Argentina and Britain.

Rosas was right. He was not obliged to answer force with force. The blockade of Buenos Aires by the Anglo-French forces so reduced trade that mercantile interests, both in Buenos Aires and in Liverpool, began to petition the British

Government for the lifting of the blockade and to circulate propaganda on Rosas' behalf. Even before the demise of the government of Sir Robert Peel, in June 1846, Lord Aberdeen was seeking the advice of River Plate hands about what to do. When Lord Palmerston returned to the Foreign Office in July 1846, he ordered an examination of what had happened in the previous five years. Although he did not immediately lift the blockade, he did order the evacuation of all British troops from Uruguay. When the British Minister in Buenos Aires on his own initiative terminated the blockade on the practical ground that it interfered with trade, Palmerston acquiesced. Shortly after, he told the French Ambassador in London that he thought the blockade an act of piracy and that England and France 'should finish in concert the bad business which they had begun together'.

A new treaty of friendship and navigation was negotiated. The island of Martín García was returned to Argentina, all Argentine ships seized during the troubles were returned with compensation for any damage done to them, and British ships of war were ordered to salute the Argentine flag as an acknowledgement of Argentine sovereignty in the waters of the Río de la Plata and its tributaries.

In 1852, General Rosas was overthrown by a combination of provincial forces under the leadership of General Justo José de Urquiza, the caudillo of Entre Ríos. For ten years, until the victory at Pavón in 1862 of the Province of Buenos Aires under General Bartolomé Mitre, political life in Argentina was very unsettled. General Urquiza succeeded, however, in creating the circumstances in which a new constitution ensured some share in decision making to provinces other than Buenos Aires. This caused the Province of Buenos Aires to separate from the Argentine Confederation. The British Government defined its policy of non-interference in the affairs of Argentina in terms of recognizing and supporting the constitutional regime of General Urquiza in his capital at Paraná. The Foreign Office resolutely refused to recognize the separate authority of Buenos Aires. Indeed, it went further and negotiated with the government at Paraná a treaty of free navigation of the rivers of Argentina, which established international free trade in all Argentine river ports, and several other powers – the United States, Brazil, Prussia, and Belgium – followed Britain's example by negotiating similar treaties of free navigation.

When, in a moment of despair, General Urquiza proposed to break up the Argentine Confederation into small separate autonomous republics, the British Minister counselled against such a course. 'We ... are interested in maintaining the Argentine Confederation,' he said, 'and in opposing by all the means which our moral influence can give, its disruption and separation.'

In spite of this policy of recognizing and doing business with the Confederation in Paraná, the British Government sent a vice-consul to Buenos Aires. Simultaneously, representatives of Baring Brothers and Company began negotiations with authorities in Buenos Aires about the repayment of the loan of 1824. The British Minister in Paraná, observing these negotiations from afar, expressed the view that a naval demonstration off Buenos Aires might hurry along a settlement. The Foreign Secretary categorically refused to listen to this suggestion. After much haggling, the representative of Barings reached an agreement with the Buenos Aires government by the terms of which the full amount of the capital of the loan was to be repaid, together with all unpaid interest. Buenos Aires refused to pay interest on unpaid interest, and Barings gave way on this point.

The inauguration of Bartolomé Mitre as President of the Argentine Republic marked the beginning of a long period of relative political calm at the centre of the community. Violence and disorder ceased to affect the vitals of society and became a frontier phenomenon on the borders of Paraguay, to the north, and in the southern pampa, where ranchers and shepherds were still threatened by the Indians. Political stability and a settled policy of developing international trade quickly became the basis of increased productive activity. In these circumstances, diplomatic intercourse between the British and Argentine governments took on a humdrum character. There were no serious problems of a political or semi-political kind.

Indeed, the very absence of problems reinforced an ignorance about Argentina in British Government circles. When in 1866 General Balcarce, the Argentine Minister in London, complained to the Foreign Secretary, the Earl of Clarendon, about articles in the British press adversely critical of business developments in the River Plate, Clarendon wrote to the British Minister in Buenos Aires asking him whether the prosperity described by General Balcarce was real or not. When told it was, Clarendon expressed his satisfaction and suggested to Balcarce that he need pay no attention to British newspapers.

Given that there were no real Anglo-Argentine problems, British diplomats and consuls were concerned to minimize the points of friction between the two countries. To this end, efforts were made to discourage emigration from Britain to Argentina on the practical grounds that any difficulties encountered by Britons in the Argentine could too easily be converted into political problems. In fact, the onset of prosperity and the increase of immigration to Argentina from the Mediterranean countries began to reduce very considerably the relative size of the British community in Argentina. In Rosas' time this community was proportionately the largest foreign community in Argentina. After 1862 it became proportionately one of the smallest, consisting mainly of businessmen, ranchers, skilled workers on the railways, and white-collar workers in banks and insurance companies.

Business activity with Argentina did, of course, generate controversy and sometimes hostility. The British Government consistently refused to assist people and interests that came into conflict with Argentine interests and with Argentine public authorities. Even when in 1880 an attempt was made by politicians in the Province of Buenos Aires to overthrow the federal government, and British ships were stopped, their cargoes seized, and commercial operations impeded, the British Government remained calm and stuck to its policy of non-interference. 'My opinion', declared the British Minister, 'is that Her Majesty's subjects who are domiciled in foreign states for their pleasure or for the purpose of earning a larger percentage of profit in business, are not exactly in the same category as British subjects at Ramsgate, Margate, Manchester or Sheffield, or other pleasure or business resorts within Her Majesty's dominions, or on board vessels carrying the British flag.' Landing marines would do more harm than good and was in any case 'illegal in the first instance and offensive to the national pride'.

It was not until the years 1890–95, however, that this policy of non-interference, in accordance with the provisions of the treaties between Britain and Argentina, was put to a significant test. As were the settled policies of the Argentine government. I refer, of course, to that climactic event in Anglo-Argentine relations – the Baring Crisis.

The Baring Crisis was brought on by the incapacity, which manifested itself in 1889, of the federal and provincial governments of Argentina to pay the interest and sinking fund charges on their foreign debt. The debt of the federal government amounted to approximately £30,000,000, and the provincial debts approximately a quarter of this sum. The prospect of default precipitated a crisis in the City of London, centring on the almost inevitable bankruptcy of Baring Brothers and Company, with consequent severe damage to the credibility of the London money market. In Argentina itself, inflation rapidly developed, investment in new projects ceased, and the tide of immigration became a tide of emigration back to Europe.

Although the crisis promised catastrophe for both Argentina and Britain, it is a curious fact that there is very little reference to it in the archives of the Foreign Office in London, and not much more in the Argentine diplomatic archives.* This is not only curious, but – like the dog that did not bark in the story by Sherlock Holmes – significant. Surely the dogs of diplomacy should have barked. One might even expect them to have turned nasty and savage. But they did not. Why?

The answer, I believe, can be divided into two parts – one Argentine, the other British. First, the Argentine solution. The

---

* There is, however, ample documentation in private archives – those of Roca and Sáenz Peña, for example.

Baring Crisis emerged in the City of London in October–November 1890. Six months before this, the crisis in the affairs of the Republic placed itself compellingly on the agenda of Argentine politics in the form of great anti-government demonstrations organized and led by the Unión Cívica, a new political grouping of young people and dissidents. In July, as a result of a real but inconclusive exchange of fire between the Navy and Army formations in Buenos Aires, the government of President Miguel Juárez Celman was replaced by that of Vice-President Carlos Pellegrini. The new government had the backing of the strong man of Argentina, General Julio A. Roca, the conqueror of the Indians of the southern pampa and President of the Republic from 1880–86 and from 1898–1904. Pellegrini and Roca were determined to do two things – preserve the place of Argentina in the international financial and trading community, and effect this on the best terms they could obtain. From the evidence I have so far examined, my conclusions are that the Argentines took the initiative in solving the crisis and that this initiative enabled the British financial community to solve its problems.

As for the British, their problems were enormous, and they were solved with finesse and by means which were, in the context of the times, new and unusual. The leading men, who together found the solution, were Thomas Lidderdale, Governor of the Bank of England; Lord Rothschild, a leading merchant banker; the Marquess of Salisbury, Prime Minister and Foreign Secretary; the Right Honourable G. J. Goschen, Chancellor of the Exchequer; the Right Honourable W. H. Smith, First Lord of the Treasury; and the Honourable John Baring. I suspect, though I cannot prove, that another important participant was G. L. Drabble, Chairman of the Bank of London and the River Plate, who had more than forty years' experience in Argentina and brought to the deliberations of the British politicians and financiers some real knowledge of the Argentines and their economy.

It must be remembered that in 1890 the Bank of England was a privately-owned, privately-controlled institution, differing from other banks only in its statutory special responsibility for the currency system under the Bank Charter Act of 1844. If it failed to meet its obligations to its creditors, the Bank of England, like any other bank, could go bankrupt. The only way to avoid such a catastrophe was for the British Government to suspend the Bank Act, thereby allowing the Bank of England to meet its obligations by printing bank notes additional to the amounts which the act authorized. As a cure, such a scheme was almost as bad as the disease it sought to remedy. Knowledge of any inadequacy in the Bank's reserves could cause creditors of all kinds to realize their assets as quickly as possible and spread panic in the money market.

As a solution this was unacceptable to Thomas Lidderdale, in whose view it would not set a good example to other banks; indeed, it would encourage bad banking and undermine the reliability of the City of London throughout the world. But he had to do something in November 1890, when the further discounting of bills endorsed by Baring Brothers and Company would inevitably lead to the bankruptcy of the Bank of England itself. The Bank could either declare its own bankruptcy or it could bankrupt Barings. For Britain, as a financial centre, either course would prove disastrous.

Lidderdale's solution was to ask the British Government not for the suspension of the Bank Act and the issue of paper currency but for an undertaking on the Government's part to share half of any loss which might be incurred by the orderly liquidation of Baring Brothers. Upon obtaining this assurance, Lidderdale invited the joint stock banks and the merchant bankers of the City to subscribe to a guarantee fund sufficient to keep Barings afloat until its assets, including the private fortunes of the Baring partners, were liquidated. The joint stock banks and the merchant banks subscribed £6,000,000 within twenty-four hours and eventually raised a sum in excess of £17,000,000. The liquidation took longer than expected, but no one, including the British Government, lost a penny.

Simultaneously, Lidderdale appointed a committee under the chairmanship of Lord Rothschild to negotiate a settlement with the Argentine government. This involved lending the Argentines substantial sums in the form of bonds in order to enable them to pay interest and sinking fund charges on their outstanding debts. Lord Rothschild argued that this was good business, for, while fresh investment in new projects in Argentina was at a standstill, production was increasing, and within a few years the country would be solvent.

As a result of the agreement with the Rothschild Committee, the Argentine foreign debt grew by nearly fifty per cent in the space of three years. This increase was accepted by the Pellegrini government, but when, as a result of a bitterly fought election, a government under Luis Sáenz Peña came to power, in December 1892, Dr C. C. Romero, the new Finance Minister, sought a fresh deal with the creditors. In a letter to *La Nación*, he declared frankly that Argentina was not paying its way in full and that the pyramiding of the foreign debt had to cease. He told the creditors that he did not wish to negotiate in London with people who knew little or nothing about Argentina but wanted a representative who spoke Spanish and understood the country. In particular, he wanted someone from Barings. As a result, the Honourable John Baring, a young man with an intimate knowledge of the Argentine, went to Buenos Aires, where he negotiated a deal which he took back to London and placed before the Rothschild Committee.

The agreement, which dealt only with the debts of the federal government, involved the payment by Argentina of £1,500,000 a year to the Bank of England, which would distribute it to the creditors. This payment would be made each year until July 1898. After this date full interest payments would be resumed, and in 1901 sinking fund repayments would recommence. The essence of the proposal was a reduction in interest payments for five years and the suspension of sinking fund payments for eight years. The Rothschild Committee accepted. In the end, Argentina resumed full interest payments a year earlier than agreed and the same for sinking fund payments.

When Lord Rothschild went to the Prime Minister, the Marquess of Salisbury, early in November 1890, to discuss the anxieties felt in the City of London about Argentina, Rothschild suggested that the Government ought to help with the problem. What form this help might take was never precisely defined. One of Rothschild's suggestions was that Argentina might benefit from policy recommendation by an outside financial adviser. Lord Salisbury remarked that this was a new idea and he would have to think about it. Such a step, he then added, would require the agreement of the Argentine Government, and a solution of this kind would preclude any expenditure by the British Government and any use of force.

Needless to say, during the years between 1890 and 1895 there were many expressions of bitterness, both in Buenos Aires and in London, about the course events were taking. Policies were adopted in Argentina to which British interests strenuously objected—for example, a tax on deposits in foreign-owned banks. Complaints were made to the British Government by various parties, but the Law Officer of the Crown, after studying these allegations, rejected them on the grounds that the taxation of foreign banks was a legitimate act of the Argentine government and that British banks could only justly protest if the taxes were levied on British-owned banks alone, in which case the British Government could raise its voice against a breach of treaty obligations. Similarly with regard to the refusal of Buenos Aires' municipal authorities to permit increases in tram fares by British-owned companies. One British official observed that the British Government would never interfere with the London County Council if it regulated the fares on foreign-owned tramways in London; conversely, he could see no reason why the British Government should interfere with the actions of the municipal authorities of Buenos Aires.

The 1890s were an age of imperialism, and the word 'intervention' was bandied about in London and in Buenos Aires as a solution to financial problems. One group of British bankers informally approached the Foreign Office with just such a suggestion. When this was brought before him in a report, Lord Salisbury wrote in red ink in the margin, 'Dreams'. A few days later, at the end of July 1891, he took the opportunity of a speech at the Mansion House to make plain the British Government's policy in Latin America.

We have no intention [he said] of constituting ourselves a Providence in any South American quarrel. We have been pressed, earnestly pressed, to undertake the part of arbitrator, of compulsory arbitrator in quarrels in the west of South America. We have been earnestly pressed also . . . to undertake the regeneration of Argentine finance. On neither of these subjects are Her Majesty's Government in the least degree disposed to encroach on the function of Providence.

The resolution of the Baring Crisis was an important factor in the inauguration of a new phase in Argentine economic development. Inflation as a feature of internal finance ceased. The peso was stabilized as a gold-backed currency. From 1899 onward, for many years the terms of international trade were favourable – sometimes extremely favourable – to Argentina. Rents, profits, and real wages rose, and the tide of investment funds began to flow once more into the economy, raising productivity and real standards of living.

Nonetheless, the Argentine government did not take this state of affairs for granted. In 1902, when Britain, Germany, and Italy combined forces to deal with the Venezuelan government on account of the treatment of foreign shipowners, sailors, and mercantile enterprises in Venezuela, Luis Drago, the Argentine Foreign Minister, raised the question, as a matter of international law, as to whether force could legitimately be used on behalf of creditor interests. This was not exactly the issue in Venezuela, and, indeed, the British Government refused to lump the interests of the Venezuelan bondholders with the losses of shipowners, sailors, and traders as part of the European claims against Venezuela. But this was not the view of the Argentine government. Drago launched a strenuous campaign to have incorporated in international law the principle that a government's foreign debts were a matter between the bondholders and the debtor government and not one which could or should be a matter for intervention by foreign governments. Some governments supported the Drago Doctrine but Britain was not one of them. In fact, the British did not use force on behalf of bondholders, and this had been conspicuously the case during the Baring Crisis, but the British were unwilling to bind their hands in such a way that they could never, in whatever circumstance, come to the assistance of creditors. There the matter rested. No difficulties ever arose in Anglo-Argentine relations to put to the test the British refusal to subscribe to the Drago Doctrine.

When World War I broke out, Argentina declared itself neutral and maintained neutrality throughout. Britain never regarded Argentine neutrality as a covertly hostile act. To them, Argentina was a source of indispensable food supplies, and to ensure these supplies the British negotiated a system of large-scale purchases. A third-generation Anglo-Argentine rancher and businessman, Herbert Gibson, became an important adviser and administrator of the British Government, and his services earned him a knighthood and eventual elevation to a baronetcy. When a series of strikes on the Argentine railways and in the docks endangered the flow of supplies, the British Minister in Buenos Aires threatened to cancel the contracts and to boycott Argentine ports. But this was bluff, the effect of which was to strengthen the will of the Argentine government to sort out its labour relations policies.

The great depression, which commenced in 1929, followed ten years later by a world war, brought to an end the Anglo-Argentine relationship that I have described as a friendship to be remembered as something far away and long ago. The mutual interdependence, manifest mainly in trade and investment, steadily diminished after World War II. This had little or nothing to do with the relative power of the two states. Indeed, the friendship here described depended upon a mutual recognition of the equivalence of power of both countries – not in the world but in the South Atlantic, where it mattered then as it does today.

If history teaches anything, the history of Anglo-Argentine relations demonstrates two general truths. First, that violence solves nothing; and second, that all issues are negotiable.

DON ROBERTO, THE WANDERING LAIRD

Alicia Jurado

The Royal Society of Arts, London
30 September 1986

Fifty years after his death in Buenos Aires in 1936, Robert Bontine Cunninghame Graham is not as well remembered in his native Scotland as he should be. His many books are out of print and almost impossible to find anywhere in Britain. In Argentina, where he was very well known in his day, the younger generations grow up perhaps without ever hearing his name. Yet in his long, adventurous life he was so many things: traveller, pioneer, rancher, aristocrat, Socialist, fencer, rider and horse lover, defender of lost causes, Scottish laird, Member of Parliament, champion of the labour movement, and last but by no means least a writer – a very able one – in spite of faults that made some of his contemporaries call him 'an amateur of genius'. A man praised by Joseph Conrad and Bernard Shaw cannot be dismissed as an insignificant writer.

In Argentina, the translations of his books into Spanish are few and virtually unobtainable, and yet how interesting we still find his descriptions of the country a century ago in those brief sketches that are his most characteristic form of narrative – Buenos Aires, when it was no more than a small provincial town; Gualeguaychú, as a mere village; the plains, raided by Indians; and the Province of Entre Ríos, threatened by lawless bands fighting each other and looting the countryside. Quite as interesting, of course, are his tales of Morocco, Spain, Paraguay, Brazil, Mexico, Colombia, or the west coast of Africa. But to the Argentines it is fascinating to imagine him riding a horse of that native breed of ours he loved so well, perhaps to a miserable fort surrounded by a ditch, which was to become the town of Azul, or taking refuge from the Indians in another mud-built fort, from which the great seaside resort of Mar del Plata would one day rise. But who was this man, and why did he travel to Argentina in 1870 to spend there what he considered, in spite of many hardships and some unpleasant adventures, the happiest days of his life?

Robert Cunninghame Graham was born in London in 1852, the son of Major William Bontine and his wife Anne Elizabeth Elphinstone Fleeming. Major Bontine did not use the name Cunninghame Graham, because there was a clause related to the inheritance of the family seat at Ardoch, in Stirlingshire, by which the eldest son was obliged to bear the name Bontine until his father's death. It is an old, illustrious family, and Robert was supposed to be the direct descendant of a king of Scotland. In fact, he used to say he had a better claim to the English throne than the Stuarts, who at some point in the family tree had succeeded to the crown in a manner that was not strictly legitimate.

The family history contains many romantic characters. There was Sir John Grahame of the Bright Sword, who died in the Battle of Falkirk in the thirteenth century, fighting with William Wallace against the English. Two centuries later, there was Sir Robert Grahame, who rebelled against his king and murdered him. There was a William Grahame, who followed Oliver Cromwell, and a Nicol Graham of Gartmore, who fought the clans of half-savage Highlanders in the eighteenth century and hung many a cattle thief upon his own gallows. He was supposed at some time to have made a prisoner of the famous Rob Roy, later immortalized by Sir Walter Scott. And there was his son, Robert Graham of Gartmore, poet and politician, who owned a sugar plantation in Jamaica and built the house in Ardoch, where our Robert – don Roberto, as he was called all over South America – lived for many years.

On his mother's side there was her father, Admiral Charles Elphinstone Fleeming, who fell in love in Cádiz with a beautiful Spanish girl when she was only fourteen – the future grandmother of don Roberto. Her fourth child, don Roberto's mother, was born on the admiral's ship off La Guaira, on the coast of Venezuela, and then afterwards lived for some time in

Caracas, where the admiral became a friend of Bolívar and Páez. Little Anne grew to be as beautiful as her Spanish mother, and at twenty-two married William Bontine, a captain in the Scots Greys. Don Roberto was their first child, and two other sons followed.

Young Robert spent most of his childhood on his father's three Stirlingshire estates – Gartmore, Ardoch, and Finlaystone. He also used to visit his Spanish grandmother, Doña Catalina, who lived with her second husband on the Isle of Wight. It was from her, of whom he was very fond, that he first learned the Spanish language, in which he was fluent.

From his earliest childhood, the boy delighted in horses and used to ride a Shetland pony in Finlaystone. His favourite home was Gartmore, in the district of Menteith, where he lived many years as a man. The place is in the Lowlands and on the border of the Highlands, so his ancestors fought constantly against the raiding clans of half-wild cattle thieves who came through the mountain passes to plunder and kill and then silently disappear into the mist. The Lake of Menteith – it is the only lake and not loch in Scotland – is nearby, with its three historic islands. Inchmahome is one, beautiful with the ruins of a medieval priory, where don Roberto's ancestors, the Earls of Menteith, are all buried and where he himself sleeps in the roofless church under the stars, as he so often slept in his travels through the vast wild lands he loved. Another is Inchtalla, where the castle was built; and the tiny Dog Island, where they used to have the kennels for the hunting pack. Don Roberto's first book, *Notes on the District of Menteith*, contains an excellent description of the place, its history, and its inhabitants, but he also wrote many stories about the Scots men and women he knew as a child, their apparent coldness and their hidden tenderness, their stoicism, their love of the land. Nobody who has read it can forget the story of the woman who, when told that her four sons had drowned together in the lake, did not say a word but went forth as usual to milk the cows. Or the one about the sick Scot, travelling by train from London to his native town, which he hoped to see once more before dying, talking to his brother about the arrangements for his own funeral with a detached interest entirely beyond the understanding of his weeping Cockney wife.

Cunninghame Graham had private tutors as a child, then went to school, and at fourteen was sent to Harrow with his brother Charles. There he appears to have been an indifferent pupil, mainly interested in sports. Two years later, his parents sent him to a school in Brussels, where he learned French – quite well as far as I can judge from the jokes and comments in that language that are to be found in many of his letters – and fencing, an art which he acquired to perfection. He then travelled in Spain, France, and Italy. His father would have liked him to join the Horse Guards, but the young man had no desire to be subjected to military discipline, and at that moment fate placed the brothers Ogilvy in his path. Edward and James Ogilvy were friends of the family. They had started breeding cattle on a ranch in the Argentine, in the Province of Entre Ríos, and wanted a partner willing to bring money into the business. Roberto's parents thought it a good idea. They gave him some capital to invest, and he sailed for Buenos Aires with James Ogilvy in 1870.

In one of Roberto's sketches, 'A Retrospect', the landing and the first glimpse of Buenos Aires are described. The port had not yet been built, and the passengers had to go ashore in boats, with their heavy luggage following in carts drawn by oxen. The town still had its old colonial look.

> The greater portion of the houses [he wrote] had flat roofs, though here and there an ugly block of modern buildings, generally overladen with detail, sprung up and dwarfed their fellows, looking like stucco icebergs in a great sea of bricks. . . .
>
> After a rainstorm, all the side streets became fierce watercourses, owing to the height of the side walks, and men with planks, which they stretched over from one pavement to the other, reaped a rich harvest from those who wished to cross.

Horse-drawn tramcars had been established shortly before, and hundreds of horses stood about hobbled in the great square round the Stock Exchange. There were few hotels, mostly near the port; foreigners usually stayed at Claraz's, kept by a Swiss, where it was highly dangerous to sit up reading late at night, because now and then a guest returning from a merry evening would attempt to shoot the candle out.

In those days few Argentines spoke English, but as he knew Spanish well Roberto was received everywhere. He went to dances that were much in the Spanish style, the ladies sitting on chairs in a great circle round the room and the men walking up to ask for a dance, perhaps a waltz, though in old-fashioned houses they still kept to the traditional dances, the *cielito* or the *pericón*. Women of the upper classes never went out alone; in the evenings, guarded by their families, they walked in Rivadavia Street, then the chief promenade of the town, pretending not to listen to the loud-voiced praises of passing men.

Roberto's next stop was Gualeguaychú, also described in detail in a sketch under that title. This small town in Entre Ríos, founded in the eighteenth century by Tomás de Rocamora by order of the Viceroy Vértiz, had remained unchanged.

Stuck like a chessboard on a table, on the plain [Roberto wrote], and with the streets all intersecting one another into squares, the houses all flat-topped and painted white, and with the towers called *miradores* looking like minarets, and the church dome resembling a mosque, it had a sort of Oriental look. The sandy unpaved streets, in which lean yellow dogs prowled after offal all the day, and howled at night in chorus at the moon, smacked also of the East. There the resemblance ended, and the line of posts, to almost every one of which a horse was tied, and the great stores, in front of which stood horses hobbled, for no one went on foot above two squares, was purely Argentine.

The ranch was a few leagues away and could only be reached on horseback. A long, low, comfortless building, it was in a perpetual state of dirtiness and disorder, owing to the fact that the Ogilvy brothers worked little and drank a great deal. Roberto began to fear he would lose his money, but he was

93

young and the sport of taming wild horses delighted him, so he began to enjoy his new life. One of his earliest photographs shows him at that period dressed in *chiripá*, poncho, *rastra*, dagger, and spurs. The *chiripá* is a kind of loin cloth; the *rastra*, a broad leather belt studded with coins.

The country as it then was is described vividly and in the greatest detail in the sketches he wrote many years later. 'La Pulpería', 'The Lazo', and 'The Bolas' provide good examples of his minute observations. The gauchos he depicts as a hardy race, more savage than the Arabs and only a step more advanced than the Indians. Tall, lean, long-haired, hospitable, and thievish, they were almost born on their horses and lived among them, talking and thinking of them, shying when they shied, as if – like centaurs – they were of one flesh.

The local customs are carefully recorded, sometimes in a story, sometimes in brief essays such as 'El Rodeo', 'Los Seguidores', and 'San José'. This last refers to the 'palace' of San José in the days of Urquiza, who was governor of Entre Ríos and ruled his subjects, in Cunninghame Graham's words,

> treating them half as children, half as savages, and they responded after the fashion of their kind, taking all leniency for weakness, and thinking power was given to a man by some wise providence which was beyond their ken.

A portrait of Urquiza hung on the wall, with the legend 'General Don Justo José de Urquiza, Napoleon of the South' written under it. The ballroom was covered with mirrors on walls and ceiling and lighted by a chandelier in which

> gilt strove with crystal for the mastery in vulgarity. . . .
> Such was the palace. Outside a Moorish-Spanish-looking house; inside a mixture of the house of a conquistador and a French brothel, and serving in itself as an apt illustration of the culture of the country under the general's rule.
> All Entre Ríos knew the place.
> Throughout that grassy, undulating Mesopotamia, shading off into forests of hard-wooded, prickly trees where it confines with Corrientes, it was a word of fear.

An interesting fact, rather to Urquiza's credit, was his protection of the local fauna. He had forbidden the hunting of rheas, deer, capybaras, and vizcachas, and the offender was dealt with as follows: the first time he was fined; the second, he was staked out between four posts with fresh hide ropes; the third, he was deprived of his horses and obliged to march among the infantry, a terrible penalty for a gaucho; and the fourth, he was put to death.

Roberto arrived shortly after Urquiza's murder by the partisans of López Jordán, who roamed the province fighting and confiscating both cattle and horses from the helpless inhabitants. Not content with this, they forced every able-bodied man they could lay hands on to join their disorganized bands and fight on their side. One day, while driving cattle to Uruguay, Roberto was met by one of those guerrilla groups and told to choose between joining them and having his throat cut. Not unnaturally, the young man chose to follow them and was obliged to remain in this enforced military service for several months, until the British consul managed to rescue him. We can read some blood-curdling stories about that period, particularly the one entitled 'A Silhouette', in which the description of a prisoner having his throat cut is written with a hair-raising realism that would seem to prove that Roberto had been an eyewitness to the event.

The experience left him undaunted, and the moment he recovered his freedom he resumed the cattle drive, taking his beasts to be sold in the south of Brazil. It was a hard life, with poor fare, half-wild cattle hands, diseases, insects, bandits, and every possible danger; but somehow the young man loved it and stored away a great deal of knowledge that was to prove invaluable to him later on, when he wrote about the Spanish conquerors and the hardships they endured in similar circumstances. He also travelled to Córdoba to sell horses and then to Mendoza, where he crossed the Andes into Chile, and finally to Paraguay, this time in search of new business opportunities.

The Paraguayan dictator Francisco Solano López was killed in 1870, after dragging his wretched country into a disastrous war against Brazil, Uruguay, and Argentina that decimated Paraguay's male population. Many years later, Cunninghame Graham was to write López's biography, *Portrait of a Dictator*. It is an excellent book, showing the tyrant – a very different figure from the hero invented by the Paraguayans in recent times – in his true light. The man was cowardly and cruel, ambitious to the verge of insanity, and so terrified of imaginary plots against him that he did not hesitate to murder his own brother and order his mother and sisters flogged on the flimsiest evidence of their having tried to deprive him of power.

Don Roberto rode from Gualeguaychú to Asunción, a tremendous distance on horseback, and became interested in the ruins of the Jesuit missions, which later inspired his book *A Vanished Arcadia*. In it, he makes good use of his first-class knowledge of the subtropical forest, its plants and animal life, and the customs of its human inhabitants. He hoped to obtain a concession from the Paraguayan government to grow *yerba mate*, a project that never materialized, because he was unable to find anyone to invest in the enterprise.

In 1872, Roberto sailed home to Gartmore, left his family dumbfounded at his new look, sunburnt, long-haired, and gaucho-like, and probably horrified his friends with dreadful stories of cruelty and bloodshed. He next visited his brother Charles, who was serving in the British Navy in Nova Scotia; there they hunted moose together and went as far as Iceland. One of Graham's best stories, 'Snaekoll's Saga', uses that frozen desert as a setting. Back in Scotland in the autumn, he returned to Argentina and Paraguay shortly afterwards, always hoping the *yerba mate* scheme would prove feasible. Finally, in despair, he gave it up and again returned home.

For a while he was conquered by civilization. He went to Paris, visited art galleries, rode in the Bois de Boulogne, fenced, took a trip to Cádiz to see his Spanish relatives and to Gibraltar to join his brother. Here he met a friend of Charles', George Mansel, a man of thirty-five who wished to retire from the Navy and do some ranching in the Province of Buenos Aires. Roberto accepted the offer to become his partner and travel with him to South America. Before leaving, however, Graham took the opportunity of sailing in a trading ship along the African coast from Morocco to Angola, watching the blacks, hating the inhuman captain, and keeping every detail in mind for a future story, 'Bristol Fashion'.

At last he and Mansel started on their voyage. When they landed in Rio de Janeiro, they found that the price of horses was much higher there than in the River Plate, so they resolved to buy a considerable number in Uruguay and drive them to Brazil. The story of this unsuccessful expedition is told in 'Cruz Alta', and we learn that after all kinds of hardship, crossing plains and mountains under sun and rain, eating dried meat, in danger of wild animals and even wilder men, plagued by insects and in constant fear of stampede, for the horses were unbroken and easily frightened, they finally reached Cruz Alta, only to learn that on account of the terrible condition of the roads they could never cross the tropical forest and get to Rio. So they had to sell their horses at the price they could fetch and return almost bankrupt to Buenos Aires.

At this point they received new funds from home and, still feeling they wanted to try their first venture, they settled at the Sauce Chico, near Bahía Blanca, in a country frequently raided by the Indians. 'Los Indios', 'The Gualichu Tree', and 'Un Angelito' are sketches that tell of this period. In the end, the inevitable happened. After a year's work, the Indians returned, destroyed the ranch, and stole the cattle. The two friends thought themselves lucky to escape to the fort of Mar del Plata with their lives.

After this experience, don Roberto was called home because of his father's failing health, but there seemed to be no danger of imminent death, for Roberto moved on again to Spain and France. In Paris, something unexpected took place. While riding in the Bois, he almost galloped into a girl who was walking there; he dismounted to apologize and appears to have fallen in love at first sight. A few days later the two eloped and, without a word to their respective families, got married in England.

The singular girl who carried him off in such unorthodox fashion went by the name of Gabrielle de la Balmondiere, claiming to be the daughter of a French father and a Spanish mother. Lady Polwarth, Cunninghame Graham's great niece and biographer, discovered only quite recently that Gabriela had been born in Yorkshire and had run away from home and a respectable family to become an actress in France. Neither pretty nor plain, in all her photographs there is an air of melancholy, but her face is grave and intelligent. She was a Catholic, deeply religious, and somewhat eccentric, for it appears that she was in the habit of roaming about the house dressed as a monk. She wrote indifferent poetry, mostly mystical, but she never seems to have gone beyond the stage of uncertainty and misery into the joys of enlightenment. There are quite good descriptions in her travel essays, and, after seven years of painstaking research in Spain, visiting convents and riding mules on rough roads in the company of her faithful Spanish maid Peregrina, she produced a scholarly book on Saint Teresa of Avila. Obsessed by death, as a result of having become a chain smoker in the days when no lady smoked at all she died at forty-five. She appears to have been gifted in many directions: she painted pleasant water-colours, was an amateur botanist, a competent bookkeeper, and also worked for the Socialist movement and for women's suffrage.

In 1879, very shortly after their marriage, the couple sailed off to New Orleans, from there travelled to Texas, and after a while settled in San Antonio, a frontier town, where every man walked about armed to the teeth. A little later they set off with mules, wagons, and a huge number of cotton bales, hoping to sell the latter at a good profit in Mexico City. This expedition is described by Gabriela in her essay 'The Waggon Train'. It was a dangerous journey on account of marauding Indians, and they had to camp at night drawing up the wagons in a circle and keeping the mules inside it. Unfortunately, the danger and discomfort brought them nothing but experience, for when they reached Mexico the price of cotton had fallen and they had to sell at a loss. To make some money, don Roberto started a fencing school under the name of Professor Bontini, enabling them to return to San Antonio with a little more to invest, but immediately our incurable optimist started another of his hopeless enterprises, a ranch on the Mexican side of the border, with a Mexican partner. This business was the shortest-lived; as was to be expected, the Indians stole all the cattle and burned the house, leaving the young couple ruined. Too proud to write home for more money, they survived by working as shop assistants. Gabriela finally went to New Orleans to teach French and painting, and Roberto stayed on driving cattle, taming horses, acting as an interpreter in buffalo hunts, and publishing short articles in a Texas newspaper, *The San Antonio Light*. Many of his future stories belong to this period, and some are extremely dramatic, such as 'Un Pelado', about a poor Mexican executed for a murder he committed with the innocence of a wild animal and who died bravely, understanding nothing.

Soon after his son and daughter-in-law returned home, Major Bontine became seriously ill and died, so Roberto came into his property and found new troubles in store. Having been somewhat mentally deranged, Major Bontine had spent money in the wildest manner, leaving Gartmore so heavily in debt that in order to save the place Roberto and Gabriela decided to live there and learn all they could about farming. It must have been a rather dull period after their frontier adventures. They never had any children, they were badly off, the large house was understaffed, and the Scottish winters cannot have helped Gabriela's melancholy. Her husband, however, went on his rounds, visited his tenants, attended the local markets, and enjoyed talking to the farm workers. The pleasure he found in describing Scottish rural types, their language and peculiarities, is obvious in many delightful sketches and short stories. Once, on a visit to Glasgow, he saw an Argentine horse drawing a tramcar, recognized the brand, and bought it. This horse, named Pampa, he rode in Hyde Park for many years and cherished its memory long after its death. He is riding Pampa in a portrait painted by John Lavery that hangs in one of the museums of Buenos Aires.

It was difficult for Cunninghame Graham to live without some form of excitement, which is perhaps what drove him into politics. About 1885, during his periodic visits to London to see his mother, he began to attend Socialist meetings, where he made friends with William Morris, Bernard Shaw, Keir Hardie, Beatrice and Sidney Webb, and others prominent in the movement. He began to shock his old friends with avant-garde notions such as the abolition of the House of Lords, universal suffrage, free education, the eight-hour working day, income tax, and so forth. How he got himself elected a Member of Parliament, in 1886, was a mystery to Bernard Shaw, but Cunninghame Graham was a remarkably good speaker and could express his opinions with elegance, simplicity, and precision, in a manner appropriate to the intellectual level of his audience. He was witty, quick in repartee, and had a fine sense of humour.

His political career was short but stormy; he must have been a thorn in the flesh of the House, for it was his habit to say exactly what he pleased, sometimes in language rather strong for his day, as he pointed out the sufferings of the poor, the low wages in factories, or the miserable conditions of both miners and their pit ponies. Nevertheless, in spite of his constant defence of the working classes, he could also laugh at his fellow-Socialists and write amusing sketches, rendering in the best Cockney their angry attacks against the existing social order.

The most spectacular feat of his political career took place on Bloody Sunday, 13 November 1887. A demonstration was organized in Trafalgar Square to obtain the freedom of some Irish patriots, but the Chief Commissioner of Police forbade it, sending a large force to cordon off the area. Graham and his friend John Burns tried to get through, and don Roberto received a blow on the head from a policeman's truncheon, ending up with a six weeks' sentence in Pentonville Prison for unlawful assembly.

At this time, Cunninghame Graham was beginning to write in earnest and went on doing so to the end of his life. He published nearly thirty books, mostly of short stories, or sketches, or descriptions of places. There were also biographies of Spanish conquistadores, such as Bernal Díaz del Castillo, Hernando de Soto, Pedro de Valdivia, and Gonzalo

Jiménez de Quesada; or of other interesting characters, like the Paraguayan dictator Francisco Solano López, the Brazilian mystic Antonio Maciel, the Venezuelan liberator José Antonio Páez, and his own ancestor, the Jamaican planter Robert Graham. We may add a couple of travel books, *Cartagena and the Banks of the Sinú* and *Mogreb-el-Acksa*. The latter is a highly entertaining account of a journey don Roberto made in Morocco, trying to reach Tarudant, a Berber town among the Atlas mountains that was forbidden to Europeans. For this expedition he disguised himself as a Turkish doctor and, barring the fact that he spoke no Turkish, quite looked the part with his pointed beard and Arab clothes, his *taleb*, or clerk, to act as interpreter, and two or three followers. But like so many of don Roberto's enterprises this one was doomed to failure; he was discovered and made a prisoner by the local governor, until he managed to smuggle out a letter to the British consul in Tangier, through whose influence Graham was at last set free. *Mogreb-el-Acksa* is not only well-written but also amusing and full of rich observation. After reading the book, Bernard Shaw used the author as the principal character in his play *Captain Brassbound's Conversion*. As well as for gauchos, Graham had a soft spot for the Arabs, and his books contain many stories about them. Their wild, primitive life, however brutal or cruel, is always placed in a favourable light when compared to Western civilization; local types are admirably portrayed, and one can feel don Roberto's deep understanding of people very different from himself. For the rest of his life, he would return to Morocco every winter; having become accustomed to warmer climates in his youth, he detested the cold of his native land.

One day, unable to continue working the estate under overwhelming debt, Roberto and Gabriela decided to sell Gartmore. It was a sad parting, but worse was to come – a few years later, Gabriela died in the south of France. Theirs had been, in a very unconventional way, a happy marriage, and don Roberto, after digging his wife's grave with his own hands in the ruined priory at Inchmahome and burying her in that unbelievably romantic place, remained inconsolable for a long time, living partly in London in a house he had found near his mother's and partly in Ardoch, another family property on the Clyde. Fortunately, don Roberto had a great number of friends, among them excellent writers like Joseph Conrad and William Henry Hudson, who were also admirers of his books.

When war broke out in 1914, Cunninghame Graham was sixty-two, but he was anxious to help his country and eventually got an appointment as head of a commission to buy horses for the War Office, and with that purpose sailed again to Buenos Aires. After an absence of thirty-six years the change in the city astonished him. Having left it little better than a village, he now found parks and palaces, fine restaurants, and fashionable men and women. In spite of his age he was still able to ride thirty miles, sleeping on the ground, throwing the lasso for hours, and mounting a bucking horse, but his greatest sorrow as he bought the fine animals he liked so much was the thought of sending them to their deaths on the battlefields of Europe.

In 1917, he was again sent on a government mission – this time to Colombia, to survey the country's cattle resources with a view to establishing a meatpacking plant. Once more he took hardships in his stride, rode many miles in a tropical climate, and travelled for days in primitive canoes. In 1925, he went to Venezuela, which he explored in very much the same way.

Cunninghame Graham devoted the last ten years of his life to the Scottish Nationalist Movement, for which he worked with his usual zeal, rushing from one meeting to another to address the public. He made other trips, including one to Ceylon and one to South Africa, but his last, in 1936, was to Argentina. Still alert and active, don Roberto was eighty-four, but catching a bad chill, which developed into pneumonia, he died at the Plaza Hotel. One of his wishes had been to see two horses, Mancha and Gato, of the native breed that had carried his friend and biographer Aimé Tschiffely from Buenos Aires to Washington on an epic fifteen-thousand-mile ride. His illness prevented this, but it is nice to remember that the crowded funeral procession escorting his remains to the ship that was to take them back to Britain was headed by

Mancha and Gato themselves, their breeder Don Emilio Solanet having sent them to Buenos Aires for the purpose.

To give a broader idea of Cunninghame Graham's many books and of his even more numerous prefaces to the books of others would require greater space than is available here. Some say he was an amateur writer, careless of his prose and with a tendency to spoil his stories with digressions on his favourite subjects. This may be true. On the other hand, once read, many of his tales remain impressed upon the memory forever. Surely, this is one of the signs of a good writer. It is also pointed out that he never invented anything and wrote only from experience. Again this is true, but a first-rate portrait is far better than feeble imitation, and his characters, whether gauchos, Arabs, Scots, Spanish prostitutes, or Texas cowboys, are so alive that you feel you have met every one of them personally. Even his biographies of the conquistadores and others, which may not be works of high scholarship, are as exciting as novels.

The painter John Lavery used to say that Cunninghame Graham's masterpiece was himself. He was, in fact, a fine human being in every respect – handsome, intelligent, kind, a bit of a dandy, perhaps, and a little vain of his remarkable appearance, but generous, friendly, brave, witty, with a sparkling sense of humour, and always ready to demand justice and to voice the grievances of the exploited and forgotten.

In Argentina his memory is dear because, after his own land, he loved no country better. In a letter now in the National Library of Scotland, he told a friend that he wanted nothing engraved upon his tomb but his name and the cattle brand he had used in his youth in Entre Ríos. Years ago, one windy autumn afternoon on the family's burial island in the Lake of Menteith, I saw that gravestone and explained to the care-taker – who could make nothing of the mysterious design from Gualeguaychú – the true meaning of a shape that to don Roberto was much more than a mere brand for cattle. To him, it was the symbol of a young, adventurous heart; of the wild, dangerous beauty he felt so attracted to – the joy of riding a half-broken horse into the unknown, and the happiest days of a long and fruitful life.

THE FICTIONS OF BORGES

Mario Vargas Llosa

The Argentine Interests Section
of the Brazilian Embassy, London
28 October 1987

As a student, I had a passion for Sartre and I firmly believed in his theses that the writer's commitment was to his own times and to the society in which he lived, that 'words were actions', and that, through writing, a man might influence history. Today such ideas seem naïve and may even invite a yawn – we live in an age of smug scepticism about the power of literature as well as about history – but in the 1950s the notion that the world could be changed for the better and that literature should contribute to this struck many of us as both persuasive and exciting.

By then, Borges' influence was beginning to be felt beyond the small circle of the magazine *Sur* and his Argentine admirers. In a number of Latin American cities, among the literary set, ardent followers fought over the scarcer editions of his books as if they were treasure and learned by heart those visionary random lists, or catalogues, that dot Borges' pages – the particularly beautiful one from 'The Aleph', for instance – and helped themselves not only to his labyrinths, tigers, mirrors, masks, and knives but also to his strikingly original use of adjectives and adverbs.

In Lima, the first of these Borges enthusiasts I came across was a friend and contemporary of mine, with whom I shared my books and my literary dreams. Borges was always an inexhaustible topic of discussion. In a clinically pure way, he stood for everything Sartre had taught me to hate: the artist shrinking from the world around him to take refuge in a world of the intellect, erudition, and fantasy; the writer looking down on politics, history, and even reality and shamelessly displaying his scepticism and his wry disdain for whatever did not stem from books; the intellectual who not only allowed himself to treat ironically the dogmas and idealism of the left but who took his own iconoclasm to the extreme of joining the Conservative Party and haughtily justifying this by claiming that gentlemen prefer lost causes.

In our discussions, I tried to show with all the Sartrean malice I could command that an intellectual who wrote, spoke, and behaved the way Borges did somehow shared responsibility for all the world's social ills, that his stories and poems were little more than *'bibelots d'inanité sonore'*, mere trinkets of high-sounding emptiness, and that History with its terrible sense of justice – which progressives wield, as it suits them, like the executioner's axe or the sharper's marked card or the conjurer's sleight of hand – would one day deal him his just deserts. But once the arguments were over, in the discreet solitude of my room or the library – like the fanatical puritan of Somerset Maugham's 'Rain', who gives in to the temptation of the flesh he renounces – I found Borges' spell irresistible. And I would read his stories, poems, and essays in utter amazement; moreover, the adulterous feeling I had that I was betraying my mentor Sartre only increased my perverse pleasure.

I have been somewhat fickle in the literary passions of my adolescence; nowadays when I reread many of the writers who were once my models, I find they no longer hold me – Sartre included. But the secret, sinful passion I harboured for Borges' work has never faded, and rereading him, which I have done from time to time like someone performing a ritual, has always been a happy experience. Only recently, in the preparation of this essay, I read all his books again, one after another, and I once more marvelled exactly as I had done the first time at the elegance and straightforwardness of his prose, the refinement of his stories, and the perfection of his craftsmanship. I am quite aware of how ephemeral literary assessment may prove, but in Borges' case I do not consider it rash to acclaim him as the most important thing to happen to imaginative writing in the Spanish language in modern times and as one of the most memorable artists of our age.

I also believe that the debt we who write Spanish owe to

Borges is enormous. That includes even those of us, like myself, who have never written a story of pure fantasy or ever felt any particular affinity with ghosts or doppelgängers, the infinite or the metaphysics of Schopenhauer. For the Latin American writer, Borges heralded the end of a kind of inferiority complex that inhibited us, all unwittingly, from broaching certain subjects and that kept us imprisoned in a provincial outlook. Before Borges, it seemed a piece of foolhardiness or self-delusion for one of us to pursue universal culture as a European or a North American might. A handful of Latin American modernist poets had previously done so, of course, but their attempts – even in the case of the most famous among them, Rubén Darío – smacked of parody, of whimsicality, something akin to a superficial, slightly frivolous journey through a foreign land. Actually, the Latin American writer had forgotten what our classical writers like the Inca Garcilaso or Sor Juana Inés de la Cruz never held in doubt, the fact that by right of language and history he was part and parcel of Western culture, not a mere epigone or a colonial but a legitimate part of that tradition, ever since Spaniard and Portuguese, four and a half centuries earlier, had extended the frontiers of Western culture to the southern hemisphere. With Borges, this became true once more; at the same time, it was proof that to participate in this culture took nothing away from the Latin American writer's sovereignty or his originality.

Few European writers have assimilated the legacy of the West as completely and thoroughly as did this Argentine poet and storyteller from the periphery. Who among Borges' contemporaries handled with equal ease Scandinavian myths, Anglo-Saxon poetry, German philosophy, Spain's Golden Age literature, the English poets, Dante, Homer, and the myths and legends of the Far and Middle East, which Europe translated and gave to the world? But this did not make a European of Borges. I remember the surprise of my students at Queen Mary College in the University of London during the 1960s – we were reading *Ficciones* and *El Aleph* – when I told them there were Latin Americans who accused Borges of being Europeanized, of being little more than an English writer. They couldn't see why. To them, this writer, in whose stories so many different countries, ages, themes, and cultural references are intertwined, seemed as exotic as the cha-cha-cha, which was all the rage at the time. They weren't wrong. Borges was not a writer imprisoned behind the heavy bars of national tradition, as European writers often are, and this facilitated his journeys through cultural space, in which, thanks to the many languages he knew, he moved with consummate ease. This cosmopolitanism, this eagerness to be a master of so far-ranging a cultural sphere, this construction of a past upon a foundation both national and foreign, was a way of being profoundly Argentine – which is to say, Latin American. But in Borges' case, his intense involvement with European literature was also a way of shaping his own personal geography, a way of being Borges. Through his broad interests and his private demons he was weaving a fabric of great originality, made up of strange combinations in which the prose of Stevenson and *The Arabian Nights*, translated by Englishmen and Frenchmen, rub shoulders with gauchos out of *Martín Fierro* and characters from Icelandic sagas; and in which two old-time hoodlums, from a Buenos Aires more imagined than remembered, fight with knives in a quarrel that seems the extension of a medieval dispute which results in the death by fire of two Christian theologians. Against the unique Borgesian backdrop, the most heterogeneous creatures and events parade – just as they do in the Aleph in Carlos Argentino Daneri's cellar. But in contrast to what takes place on that tiny passive screen, which can reveal the elements of the universe only at random, in Borges' work every element and every being is brought together, filtered through a single point of view and given the verbal expression that lends it individual character.

Here is another area in which the Latin American writer owes much to the example of Borges. Not only did he prove to us that an Argentine could speak with authority on Shakespeare and create convincing stories with characters who hailed from Aberdeen, but he also revolutionized the tradition of his literary language. Note that I said 'example'

and not 'influence'. Borges' prose, because of its wild originality, has wreaked havoc amongst countless admirers, in whose
work the use of certain images or verbs or adjectives established by him turns into mere parody. This is the most readily
detectable influence, for Borges was one of the writers who
managed completely to put his own personal stamp on the
Spanish language. 'Word music' was his term for it, and it is as
distinctive in him as it is in the most illustrious of our classics –
namely Quevedo, whom Borges admired, and Góngora,
whom he did not. Borges' prose is so recognizable to the ear
that often in someone else's work a single sentence or even a
simple verb ('*conjeturar*', for example, or '*fatigar*' used tran-
sitively) becomes a dead giveaway of Borges' influence.

Borges made a profound impression on Spanish literary
prose, as before him Rubén Darío had on poetry. The difference between them is that Darío imported and introduced
from France a number of mannerisms and themes that he
adapted to his own world and to his own idiosyncratic style. In
some way all this expressed the feelings, and at times the
snobbery, of a whole period and a certain social milieu. Which
is why his devices could be used by so many without his
followers losing their individual voices. The Borges revolution
was personal. It represented him alone, and only in a vague,
roundabout way was it connected with the setting in which he
was formed and which in turn he helped crucially to form –
that of the magazine *Sur*. Which is why in anyone else's hands
Borges' style comes across as a caricature.

But this clearly does not diminish his importance or lessen in
the slightest the enormous pleasure his prose gives. It can be
savoured, word by word, like a delicacy. The revolutionary
thing about Borges' prose is that it contains almost as many
ideas as words, for his precision and concision are absolute.
While this is not uncommon in English or French literature, in
Hispanic literature it has few precedents. Marta Pizarro, a
character in Borges' story 'The Duel', reads Lugones and
Ortega y Gasset, and this confirms 'her suspicion that the
language to which she had been born was less fit for expressing
the mind or the passions than for verbal showing off.' Joking

aside, if we omit what she says about the passions there is some truth to her remark. Like Italian or Portuguese, Spanish is a wordy language, bountiful and flamboyant, with a formidable emotional range, but for these same reasons it is conceptually inexact. The work of our greatest prose writers, beginning with Cervantes, is like a splendid display of fireworks in which every idea marches past preceded and surrounded by a sumptuous court of servants, suitors, and pages, whose function is purely decorative. In our prose, colour, temperature, and music are as important as ideas, and in some cases – Lezama Lima, for example – more so. There is nothing objectionable about these typically Spanish rhetorical excesses. They express the profound nature of a people, a way of being in which the emotional and the concrete prevail over the intellectual and the abstract. This is why Valle-Inclán, Alfonso Reyes, Alejo Carpentier, and Camilo José Cela, to cite four magnificent prose writers, are so verbose in their writing. This does not make the prose either less skilful or more superficial than that of a Valéry or a T. S. Eliot. They are simply quite different, just as Latin Americans are different from the English and the French. To us, ideas are formulated and captured more effectively when fleshed out with emotion and sensation or in some way incorporated into concrete reality, into life. Far more than they are in a logical discourse. This, perhaps, is why we have such a rich literature and such a dearth of philosophers. The most illustrious thinker in the Spanish language in modern times, Ortega y Gasset, is above all a literary figure.

Within this tradition, Borges' prose is an anomaly, for, in opting for the strictest frugality, he deeply disobeys the Spanish language's natural tendency towards excess. To say that with Borges Spanish became intelligent may appear offensive to other writers of the language, but it isn't. What I am trying to say in the wordiness I have just described is that in Borges there is always a logical, conceptual level to which all else is subservient. His is a world of clear, pure, and at the same time unusual ideas that, while never relegated to a lower plane, are expressed in words of great directness and restraint. 'There is no more elaborate pleasure than that of thought, and we surrendered ourselves to it,' says the narrator of 'The Immortal' in words that give us a perfect picture of Borges. This story is an allegory of his fictitious world; in it, the intellectual always devours and destroys the mere physical.

In forging a style of this kind, which so genuinely reflected his taste and background, Borges made a radical innovation in the stylistic tradition of Spanish. By purifying it, by intellectualizing and colouring it in such a personal way, he showed that the language, about which – like his character Marta Pizarro – he was often so severe, was potentially much richer and more flexible than tradition seemed to indicate. Provided that a writer of Borges' calibre attempted it, Spanish was capable of becoming as lucid and logical as French and as straightforward and full of nuances as English. There is no other work in our language like Borges' to teach us that with regard to literary Spanish there is always more to be done, that nothing is final and permanent.

The most intellectual and abstract of our writers at the same time was a superb storyteller. One reads most of Borges' tales with the hypnotic interest usually reserved for reading detective fiction, a genre he was to cultivate while injecting it with metaphysics. But his attitude to the novel was one of scorn. Predictably, its realistic tendencies troubled him, because, with the exception of Henry James and a few other illustrious practitioners, the novel is a genre that resists being bound to what is purely speculative and artistic and so is condemned to melt into the sum total of human experience – ideas and instincts, the individual and society, reality and fantasy. The novel's congenital imperfection, its dependence on human clay, Borges found intolerable. This is why, in 1941, he wrote in the foreword to *The Garden of Branching Paths* that 'the habit of writing long books, of extending to five hundred pages an idea that can be perfectly stated in a few minutes' time, is a laborious and exhausting extravagance.' The remark takes for granted that every book is an intellectual discourse, the expounding of a thesis. If that were true, the details of any work of fiction would be little more than superfluous garments on a handful of concepts, which could be isolated and extracted like the pearl that nests in the shell. Can *Don Quixote, Moby Dick, The Charterhouse of Parma, The Devils* be reduced to one or two ideas? Borges' statement is not useful as a definition of the novel but it does reveal to us, eloquently, that the central concern of his fiction is conjecture, speculation, theory, doctrine, and sophism.

Owing to its brevity and compression, the short story was the genre most suited to those subjects that prompted Borges to write. Time, identity, dreams, games, the nature of reality, the double, eternity – thanks to his mastery of the craft – lost their vagueness and abstraction and took on charm and even a sense of drama. These preoccupations appear ready-made as stories, usually starting cleverly with quite realistic, precise details and footnotes, often concerned with local colour, so that at some point; imperceptibly or even brusquely, he can steer them towards the fantastic or make them vanish in philosophical or theological speculation. Never important or truly original in these tales are the facts; but the theories that explain them and the interpretations that they give rise to are. For Borges, just as for his ghostly character in 'Utopia of a Tired Man', facts 'are mere points of departure for invention and reasoning.' Reality and fantasy are fused through the style and through the ease with which the narrator moves from one to the other, more often than not displaying devastatingly sardonic erudition and an underlying scepticism that keeps in check any undue indulgence.

In a writer as sensitive as Borges and in a man as courteous and frail as he was – especially since his growing blindness made him little more than an invalid – the amount of blood and violence to be found in his stories is astonishing. But it shouldn't be. Writing is a compensatory activity, and literature abounds in cases like his. Borges' pages teem with knives, crimes, and scenes of torture, but the cruelty is kept at a distance by his fine sense of irony and by the cold rationalism of his prose, which never falls into sensationalism or the purely emotional. This lends a statuesque quality to the physical horror, giving it the nature of a work of art set in an unreal world.

Borges was always fascinated by the mythology and the stereotype of the hoodlum of the outer slums of Buenos Aires and the knife fighter of rural Argentina. These hard-bitten men, with their sheer physicality, animal innocence, and unbridled instincts, were his exact opposites. Yet he peopled a number of his stories with them, bestowing on them a certain Borgesian dignity – that is to say, an aesthetic and intellectual quality. It is obvious that these thugs, knife fighters, and cruel murderers of his invention are as literary – as unreal – as his characters of pure fantasy. The former may wear ponchos or speak in a way that apes the language of old-time hoodlums or gauchos from the interior, but none of this makes them any more realistic than the heresiarchs, magicians, immortals, and scholars who inhabit his stories, either today or in the remote past, from every corner of the globe. All have their origins not in life but in literature. All are, first and foremost, ideas magically made flesh, thanks to the expert spinning of words by a great literary conjurer.

Each one of Borges' stories is an artistic jewel and some, like 'Tlön, Uqbar, Orbis Tertius', 'The Circular Ruins', 'The Theologians,' and 'The Aleph', are masterpieces of the genre. The unexpectedness and subtlety of his themes are matched by an unerring sense of structure. Obsessively economical, Borges never admits a word or a scrap of information that is superfluous, although to tax the reader's ingenuity details are sometimes left out. The exotic is an indispensable element. Events take place far removed in space or time, and this distancing gives them an added allure. Or else they occur in the legendary outer slums of old-time Buenos Aires. In a remark about one of his characters, Borges says, 'The fellow . . . was a Turk; I made him into an Italian so that I could more easily fathom him.' In fact, Borges usually did the opposite. The more removed in time or space his characters were from him or his readers, the better he could manipulate them, attributing to them those marvellous qualities with which they are endowed or making their often improbable experiences more convincing. But this is not to say that Borges' exoticism and local colour have a kinship with the exoticism and local colour of regionalist writers like Ricardo Güiraldes and Ciro Alegría. In their work the exoticism is spontaneous and stems from a narrowly provincial, localized vision of the countryside and its customs, which the regionalist writer identifies with the world. In Borges, the exoticism is a pretext. He uses it, with the approval or the ignorance of the reader, to slip rapidly, imperceptibly, out of the real world and into that state of unreality which, in common with the hero of 'The Secret Miracle', Borges believes 'is the prerequisite of art'.

An inseparable complement to the exoticism in his stories is the erudition, the bits of specialized knowledge, usually literary but also philological, historical, philosophical, or theological. This knowledge, which borders on but never oversteps the bounds of pedantry, is quite freely flaunted. But the point of it is not to show off Borges' wide acquaintance with different cultures. Rather, it is a key element in his creative strategy, the aim of which was to imbue his stories with a certain colourfulness, to endow them with an atmosphere all their own. In other words, Borges' learning, like his use of exotic settings and characters, fulfils an exclusively literary function, which, in twisting the erudition around and making it sometimes decorative, sometimes symbolic, subordinates it to the task at hand. In this way, Borges' theology, philosophy, linguistics, and so forth lose their original character, take on the quality of fiction, and, becoming part and parcel of a literary fantasy, are turned into literature.

'I'm rotten with literature,' Borges once confessed in an interview. So was his fictional world. It is one of the most literary worlds any author ever created. In it, the words, characters, and myths forged down through the years by other writers flock in and out, over and over, and so vividly that they somehow encroach on the objective world, which is the usual context of any literary work. The reference point in Borges' fiction is literature itself. 'Little has happened to me in my lifetime, but I have read much,' Borges wrote teasingly in his afterword to *Dreamtigers*. 'Or, rather, little has happened more memorable than the philosophy of Schopenhauer or the word music of England.' This should not be taken too literally, for any man's life, however uneventful, conceals more riches and mystery than the profoundest poem or the most complex mental processes. But the remark reveals a subtle truth about the nature of Borges' art, which, more than that of any other modern writer, comes of metabolizing world literature and putting an individual stamp on it. His brief narratives are full of resonances and clues that stretch away to the four cardinal points of literary geography. It is to this no doubt that we owe the zeal of the practitioners of heuristic literary criticism, who are tireless in their attempts to track down and identify Borges' endless sources. Arduous work it is too, make no mistake, and what's more it is pointless, for what lends greatness and originality to Borges' stories are not the materials he used but what he turned those materials into: a small imaginary world, populated by tigers and highly educated readers, full of violence and strange sects, acts of cowardice and uncompromising heroism, in which language and imagination replace objective reality, and the intellectual task of reasoning out fantasies outshines every other form of human activity.

It is a world of fantasy, but only in the sense that it contains supernatural beings and abnormal events, not in the sense that it is an irresponsible world, a game divorced from history and even from mankind. There is much that is playful in Borges, and on the fundamental questions of life and death, human destiny and the hereafter, he expresses more doubt than certainty, but his is not a world separated from life or from everyday experience or without roots in society. Borges' work is as grounded in the changing nature of existence – that common predicament of the human species – as any literary work that has lasted. How could it be otherwise? No work of fiction that turns its back on life or that is incapable of illuminating life has ever attained durability. What is singular about Borges is that in his world the existential, the historical, sex, psychology, feelings, instincts, and so forth have been dissolved and reduced to an exclusively intellectual dimension. And life, that boiling chaotic turmoil, reaches the reader sublimated and conceptualized, transformed into literary myth through the filter of Borges – a filter of such perfect logic that it sometimes appears not to distil life to its essence but to suppress it altogether.

Poetry, short story, and essay are all complementary in Borges' work, and often it is difficult to tell into which genre a particular text of his fits. Some of his poems tell stories, and many of his short stories – the very brief ones especially – have the compactness and delicate structure of prose poems. But it is mostly in the essay and short story that elements are switched, so that the distinction between the two is blurred and they fuse into a single entity. Something similar happens in Nabokov's novel *Pale Fire*, a work of fiction that has all the appearance of a critical edition of a poem. The critics hailed the book as a great achievement. And of course it is. But the truth is that Borges had been up to the same sort of tricks for years – and with equal skill. Some of his more elaborate stories, like 'The Approach to al-Mu'tasim', 'Pierre Menard, the Author of Don Quixote', and 'An Investigation of the Works of Herbert Quain', pretend to be book reviews or critical articles.

In the majority of his stories, invention, the forging of a make-believe reality, follows a tortuous path, cloaking the tales in historical re-creation or in philosophical or theological inquiry. Since Borges always knows what he's saying, the intellectual groundwork for this sleight of hand is quite solid, but exactly what is fictitious in his stories remains ambiguous. Lies masquerade as truths and vice versa – this is typical of Borges' world. The opposite may be said of many of his essays, such as 'A History of Eternity' or the little pieces in his *Book of Imaginary Beings*. In them, amongst the scraps of basic knowledge upon which they rest, an added element of fantasy and unreality, of pure invention, filters through like a magic substance and turns them into fiction.

No literary work, however rich and accomplished it may be, is without its darker side. In the case of Borges, his work sometimes suffers from a certain cultural ethnocentricity. The black, the Indian, the primitive often appear in his stories as inferiors, wallowing in a state of barbarism apparently unconnected either to the accidents of history or to society but inherent in their race or status. They represent a lower humanity shut off from what Borges considered the greatest of all human qualities – intellect and literary refinement. None of this is explicitly stated, and doubtless it was not even conscious; rather, it shows through in the slant of a certain sentence or may be deduced from observation of a particular mode of behaviour. For Borges, as for T. S. Eliot, Giovanni Papini, and Pio Baroja, civilization could only be Western, urban, and almost – almost – white. The East survives, but only as an appendage – that is, as it has come down to us through the filter of European translations of Chinese, Persian, Japanese, or Arabic originals. Those other cultures that form part of Latin America – the native Indian and the African – feature in Borges' world more as a contrast than as different varieties of mankind. Perhaps this is because they were a meagre presence in the milieu in which he lived most of his life. It is a limitation that does not detract from Borges' many other admirable qualities, but it's best not to sidestep it when giving a comprehensive appraisal of his work. Certainly it is a limitation that offers further proof of his humanity, since, as has been said over and over again, there is no such thing as absolute perfection in this world – not even in the work of a creative artist like Borges, who comes as close as anyone to achieving it.

JUAN LÓPEZ AND JOHN WARD

Jorge Luis Borges

Translated by
Norman Thomas di Giovanni

It was their fate to live in strange times.

The world had been parcelled up into different countries, each furnished with loyalties, cherished memories, a clearly heroic past, rights and wrongs, its own mythology, its luminaries in bronze, its national holidays, demagogues, and emblems. These divisions, so dear to the map maker, held the seeds of war.

López had been born in the city beside the unmoving river; Ward, in a suburb of the city that had known the footsteps of Father Brown. To read *Don Quixote*, Ward had studied Spanish. The other young man had a passion for Conrad, who had been revealed to him in a lecture hall in Viamonte Street.

The two might have become friends, but they met face to face only once, on some far too notorious islands, and each of them was Cain, and each Abel.

They were buried in the same grave. Frozen ground and corruption know them.

The events I relate took place in a time it is given none of us to understand.

NOTES ON CONTRIBUTORS

JORGE LUIS BORGES, one of the great masters of prose fiction of our time, was born in Buenos Aires in 1899 and died in Geneva in 1986. He came of English stock on his father's side, and not only grew up speaking two languages but also from a very early age was steeped in the literary worlds of both contemporary Argentina and – thanks to his father's passion for English poets – nineteenth-century Great Britain. Borges won early fame as a poet with the publication of his first book, *Fervor de Buenos Aires*, in 1923, and then as an essayist; he did not, in fact, begin writing short stories until he was in his late thirties, but his first book in that genre, *El jardín de los senderos que se bifurcan* (The Garden of Branching Paths), published in 1942, must truly rank as one of the most revolutionary literary works of the century. The volume was expanded in 1944, when it appeared as *Ficciones*. Perhaps his finest work is contained in *El Aleph* (1949; enlarged 1952), a further set of stories. Borges became Director of the Argentine National Library on the downfall of Perón in 1955, a post he held until Perón's putative return to power in 1973. The year of his appointment as librarian also marked the onset of Borges' increasing blindness, an inherited affliction which turned him back to composing poetry and which for seventeen years prevented him from writing more than one short story.

Borges received his formal education in Geneva, during the years of the First World War, and there he learned French and German. Later, in Spain, he studied Latin. Although he was without a university degree himself, in 1956 he became Professor of English and American Literature at the University of Buenos Aires. Some of his other noteworthy titles are the sketches *Historia universal de la infamia* (A Universal History of Infamy), 1935; the essays *Otras Inquisiciones 1937–52* (Other Inquisitions); and the late story collections *El informe de Brodie* (Doctor Brodie's Report) and *El libro de arena* (The Book of Sand), published, respectively in 1970 and 1975.

In his last years, Borges wrote less but travelled widely, lecturing, conversing, and receiving numerous literary awards and academic distinctions. His first among many honorary degrees in the English-speaking world was that conferred by Columbia University in 1971; he also received degrees from Oxford that same year, and from Cambridge in 1984. His international prizes included the Formentor, the Matarazzo, the Jerusalem, the Cervantes, and the Cino del Duca. Borges' influence has been broad; he also acknowledged the influence on him of such writers as Kipling, Stevenson, Chesterton, and the panoply of authors responsible for the Eleventh Edition of the *Encyclopædia Britannica*. Borges' other literary interests, taken up in his maturity, were Old English poetry and the Norse sagas. He left a series of valuable collections of radio talks, in the form of conversations with the young poet Osvaldo Ferrari, which belong to the last three years of his life.

NORMAN THOMAS DI GIOVANNI worked with Borges in Cambridge, Massachusetts, and in Buenos Aires from the end of 1967 to 1972. To date, he has produced translations of ten of Borges' books in English – a number of them in collaboration with their author – including two of poetry, two of essays, and six of short fiction. An American by birth, di Giovanni has lived in Britain since 1972, currently in Devon. He has also translated stories and novels of other Argentine authors and is compiling three different anthologies of their work as well as writing a book on his association with Borges.

H. S. FERNS was born in Calgary, Alberta, in 1913, and was educated at the University of Manitoba and at Trinity College, Cambridge, where he became a Research Scholar in 1938. He served on the staff of the Canadian Prime Minister in 1940, and was Assistant Professor of History and Government at Manitoba before being appointed to a lectureship in Modern History and Government at the University of Birmingham in 1950. He held the chair of Political Science at Birmingham from 1961 to 1981 and is now Emeritus Professor. Among his publications are *Britain and Argentina in the Nineteenth Century* (1960), *Argentina* (1969), and *The Argentine Republic 1516–1971* (1973), as well as numerous articles in learned journals. He lives in Birmingham.

GRAHAME GREENE is the English world's foremost living practitioner of the art of fiction. Born in 1904, he is the author of numerous novels, short stories, essays, plays, film scripts, travel books, and books for children. He was educated at Berkhamsted School and Balliol College, Oxford. Since the publication of his novel *Stamboul Train* in 1932, he has, unusually, achieved both critical and popular acclaim. Several of his fictional works have Latin American backgrounds, including *The Power and the Glory* (Mexico), *Our Man in Havana* (Cuba), *The Comedians* (Haiti), *The Honorary Consul* (Argentina); as do two non-fiction titles, *The Lawless Roads* (Mexico) and *Getting to Know the General* (Panama). He was made a Companion of Honour in 1966 and received the Order of Merit in 1986. In 1977, he served as a member of the Panamanian delegation to Washington for the signing of the Canal Treaty; five years later, the government of Panama awarded him the Grand Cross, Order of Vasco Núñez de Balboa.

ALICIA JURADO, the Argentine novelist and biographer, was born in Buenos Aires in 1922, and, despite a doctorate in biology from the University of Buenos Aires, has always followed a career in writing. She is the author of four novels: *La cárcel y los hierros* (1961), *En soledad vivía* (1967), *El cuarto mandamiento* (1974) and *Los hechiceros de la tribu*

(1980); and two story collections: *Leguas de polvo y sueño* (1965) and *Los rostros del engaño* (1968). As well as the lives of W. H. Hudson and R. B. Cunninghame Graham, she has written a critical biography of Borges, *Genio y Figura de Jorge Luis Borges*, published in 1964, ten years after she first met him. She also wrote with him a short work on Buddhism, *Qué es el Budismo* (1976). Her books have won several prizes, and she has held fellowships from both the Guggenheim and Fulbright foundations and from the British Council. Since 1980, Alicia Jurado has been one of the twenty-four members of the Argentine Academy of Letters.

MARIO VARGAS LLOSA's mark on Latin American writing during the last twenty years has been nothing short of phenomenal. Author of some of the most complex and highly respected novels of our time, he has produced a long and impressive list of fictional work: *The Time of the Hero, The Green House, The Cubs and Other Stories, Conversation in the Cathedral, Captain Pantoja and the Special Service, Aunt Julia and the Script Writer, The War of the End of the World, The Real Life of Alejandro Mayta*, and the recent *Who Killed Palomino Molero?* In addition, he is a playwright, the author of major studies of Gabriel García Márquez and Gustave Flaubert, and a prolific literary journalist and polemicist. From 1976 to 1979, he served as President of International PEN. Born in Arequipa, Peru in 1936, Vargas Llosa studied at San Marcos University, in Lima, and later at the University of Madrid. He went to Paris in 1959, where he worked for a French news agency and French radio. He travelled to Cuba in 1962, returning there three years later as a member of the prestigious Casa de las Américas prize jury. In 1971, he repudiated the Cuban revolution and in 1974 returned to live in Lima. He was appointed by the Peruvian government in 1983 to investigate the Ayacucho massacre. The next year he was offered, but declined, the post of prime minister. His novel *The Green House* won the first Rómulo Gallegos Prize, in Caracas in 1967. He now lives part of the year in London.